# SHAKESPEARE
# AND HIS PLAYS

The author presents the few known facts and
some of the legends about Shakespeare the man,
against the background of sixteenth and early
seventeenth-century England. He then rapidly
surveys the 'works', giving a brief sketch of the
story of most of the Plays, with a few comments
aimed at helping his readers to discover for
themselves something of the magic which has
held the world captive for over 300 years. After
touching on the fascinating history of the 'text'
of Shakespeare Mr. Burton discusses some of
the elements of Shakespeare's genius.

The essence of an 'Outline' is that it can be
filled in, and Mr. Burton's aim has been to
encourage his readers to supplement this brief
introduction to a vast subject by reading the
Plays and whenever possible seeing them acted.
His emphasis is on two main aspects: the man
Shakespeare—the practical man of the theatre
at work—and the essential realization that the
Plays were written to be acted.

Mr. Burton's lifelong study of Shakespeare,
and his experience—as teacher, broadcaster,
amateur actor and producer of Shakespeare's
Plays—enable him to present his subject to
young readers with sympathy and understanding but without condescension.

Martin Droeshout sculpsit London.

*Shakespeare*

# SHAKESPEARE
## and his Plays

BY

## H. M. BURTON

*with illustrations to the plays by*
RICHARD G. ROBINSON

ROY PUBLISHERS NEW YORK

*First published* 1958
*Reprinted* 1959

© 1958 H. M. Burton

Library of Congress Catalogue
Card No. 59–5652
PRINTED IN GREAT BRITAIN

# Contents

## NOTE ON THE PORTRAIT OF SHAKESPEARE

This is taken from the woodcut by Martin Droeshout on the title-page of the First Folio, 1623. It was commissioned by Shakespeare's friends and is therefore probably a good likeness. But it seems likely that the engraver had only a drawing of the head to work from, for the doublet is badly drawn. Indeed, some critics have suggested that it shows two left arms, a hint to those in the know that the man here portrayed was not the true author of the plays published under his name.

# Introduction

There are some people who say they "don't like Shakespeare". They might just as well say they don't like winter, or air-travel, or television. These things are part of our existence and so, whether we "like" him or not, is Shakespeare. He is as important a figure in the history of mankind as Nelson or Lincoln, Newton or Einstein. His works have become a part of us and if they had never been written our lives and our language would have been so much the poorer. Most of those who "don't like Shakespeare" have probably never had a chance to decide fairly whether they do or not. They may have studied one of his plays at school for an examination or at the mercy of an unimaginative teacher. They may have tried to read a play or two for themselves and been frightened off by the unfamiliar language. But Shakespeare wrote his plays to be acted, not to be studied or even read. Anybody who has seen one or two of them well produced on the stage, and has still come away not "liking" Shakespeare must be exceptional. In any case he should realise that he has the opinion of men and women throughout the world, as well as the verdict of history, against him.

Except for a period in the 17th century (when the public were not allowed to see Shakespeare's plays as he wrote them because they were altered) there has never been a time when Shakespeare has lost his hold on the theatre. Somewhere or other in the English-speaking world, for two hundred years or so, his plays have been continuously "in production"—and that is true of no other dramatist the world has known.

You cannot explain away genius; you can only read, and learn—and wonder.

# I. The Age

### A TIME OF CHANGE

We always think and write of Shakespeare as an Elizabethan but it is worth noticing that he died in 1616, which was thirteen years after the death of Queen Elizabeth I. As he was born in 1564 he was under forty when James I became king and nine or ten of his greatest plays were written in King James's reign. However, it was the great Elizabethan Age that made him and before we begin to study the man and his work it might be interesting to look at the England which he knew as a boy and as a young man.

### RELIGION AND TRADE

First of all, then, Elizabethan England was a land of great and exciting change. Of course it is much easier to see that now, looking back on it after more than three hundred years; but even at the time some of the changes must have been apparent to ordinary people. They would know, for example, that during the previous fifty or sixty years the "official" religion of the country had changed from Roman Catholicism to Protestantism, then back to Roman Catholicism during the reign of Mary Tudor and back to Protestantism again with Queen Elizabeth. They would also know—especially if they lived near London or some other sea-port—that English ships were fighting and trading in foreign waters more often, and more successfully, than ever before. Even to the remote country towns and villages would come, every now and then, some old sailor with tales of wonder and delight, or some new commodity for sale on the chapman's packhorse—silk, or an eastern rug, a new kind of scent, or a new spice; ginger, perhaps, or tobacco! It is

2

difficult for us today to realise the thrill of excitement with which the ordinary men and women greeted these new things for the first time in the sixteenth century.

But there were other changes which were going on all the time although ordinary men and women probably knew little about them. For centuries England had been divided, in more ways than one. It had been the scene of civil wars between powerful groups of rich landowners, which divided the nation in one way; but it had also been divided up into hundreds of towns and villages which were all more or less separate from each other—there was no sense of belonging to a particular county, let alone a particular country. Londoners, and perhaps a sprinkling of gentry and clergy up and down the country, might think of "England" with feelings of pride, but it was not until the sixteenth century that this feeling began to spread to people in all walks of life. The victory against the Spanish Armada did more than defeat Spain: it helped to weld England into a nation. With the accession of James I came the complete union of England (and Wales) with Scotland, which did still more to foster the patriotic spirit of the nation.

### THE NEW LEARNING

The next great change was not peculiar to this country; it was common to most of Western Europe and is known as the Renaissance, or the Revival of Learning. You probably know more about that than the majority of grown-up men and women knew in Elizabethan days, but it was a change which affected the daily lives of everybody. Had you been living then you would probably have noticed that schools were springing up in every town of any size, that rich men were founding hospitals and building alms-houses, that more and more books and pamphlets (which you would have called "broadsides" or "broadsheets") were appearing in shops or on the travelling chapman's trays—and there were far more people every year who were able to read. You would have seen beautiful new houses being built, and many of your friends would be learning to play musical instruments or to sing quite difficult part-songs. But despite all these new things going on all round you it is very doubtful if you would ever have heard anybody mention the Renaissance, or the Revival of Learning.

### SHAKESPEARE, THE MAN OF HIS AGE

There were giants in the land in those days! The Queen herself was a genius in her own way. Then there were the great navigators and sea-captains—Drake and Raleigh and Hawkins. It seems as if the exploits and discoveries of these men inspired the men of thought to rival the men of action. Francis Bacon was one of the greatest of all philosophers and lawyers; Hooker was one of the greatest of all theological scholars; Spenser was one of the greatest English poets; Cecil was one of the greatest English statesmen; so we could go on. And all these men were the product of the Elizabethan Age, the great age of change and revolution. So was Shakespeare, our greatest dramatist.

### CONTRASTS

But besides being an age of change, it was also an age of contrasts. The men and women who took such pleasure in singing madrigals and playing stringed instruments in small orchestras on, say, Monday and Friday evenings, might go to the bull-ring or the bear-pit on Wednesdays and Saturdays, where they would see wretched animals, filthy and mangey, chained to a pole and set on by fierce and hungry dogs. The smart young man going to visit a friend down the river at Deptford would slip a book of sonnets or love-poems into his pocket to read, and then direct his boatman to take him round by Execution Dock so that he might take another look at the rotting bodies of pirates who were hanged there and left to decay for three tides. An entirely respectable family—say mother, father and three little children—would wait for hours at Tyburn to get a good seat for a public execution, which might include ghastly horrors like the disembowelling of the victim while he was still alive. These things were not considered shocking or degrading; the Queen herself often visited the bear-garden.

But there were other kinds of contrast. Side by side with the great houses and halls which the Elizabethans were building in London and other cities there were dark and insanitary hovels crowded with human beings. The streets were little more than narrow, rutted tracks, often with an open sewer beside them, and even the Strand was a muddy lane running behind the great palaces on the river bank. A fairly prosperous tradesman might dress himself in beautiful clothes to visit friends—and have to skirt a reeking pile of refuse outside his front door as he left the house. (Shakespeare's father, a respected citizen of Stratford-

*Heads on London Bridge Gate, through which Shakespeare must often have passed. From Visscher's View of London,* 1661

on-Avon, was fined for not clearing away such an obstruction before his house.) The story of Sir Walter Raleigh's throwing down his cloak over a puddle for the Queen to walk on may not be strictly true, but it gives some idea of the state of the roads at the time—and it was a typical Elizabethan gesture of gallantry.

We are constantly being reminded of these contrasts as we see or read Shakespeare's plays. *Macbeth* is a tragedy, full of noble and beautiful poetry; yet at the height of the tragedy the bleeding head of Macbeth is brought on to the stage.

4

Today we regard such a sight as horrible but the Elizabethans were used to seeing the heads of traitors and others cut off and held high by the executioner for all to see. King Lear refers, without expressing disapproval or surprise, to the public whipping of women in London—and *King Lear* is one of the most moving and beautifully written of Shakespeare's tragedies. (In passing, we might notice that Lear was supposed to live in ancient Britain, whereas the whipping of women to which he refers took place in Shakespeare's own day; but that kind of mistake, called an anachronism, never worried Shakespeare or his audience, and it need not worry us.)

### "MERRY ENGLAND"

There was another aspect of Elizabethan England which we find reflected in Shakespeare's plays. It was—and still is—called "Merry England". Not long after Shakespeare's death the very strict Puritans were to put an end to a great deal of the gaiety which he had observed and enjoyed, but that was still in the future (although Shakespeare, in *Twelfth Night*, portrayed a Puritan kill-joy—the steward Malvolio). We read in his plays of all the games, sports and other happy pastimes which were popular—bowls, archery, hunting, hawking, dancing and singing, to say nothing of the crueller sports we have mentioned. But from our point of view, in considering how far Shakespeare was the product of the Elizabethan Age, perhaps the most important pastime was play-acting. There must have been a certain amount of amateur acting; the rustic players of *A Midsummer Night's Dream*, although

they were supposed to be playing in ancient Greece, were obviously drawn from country players whom Shakespeare had seen, while at the Court, and in the country houses of the rich there were most elaborate performances of short plays with music called "Masques", in which the parts were taken by the ladies and gentlemen present. But the professional theatre was also flourishing.

### THE DRAMA IN ENGLAND

In earlier days the plays had been closely connected with Church festivals and were based on Bible stories. As time went on they became rather too rowdy and coarse for the Church, although they were still based roughly on the same stories. Then the Guilds took a hand and provided separate scenes for elaborate "pageants" on feast days and saints' days. In Elizabeth's reign there were groups of young actors formed by the choir-boys of St. Paul's Cathedral and other great churches, and special plays were written for them. For many years these boys' companies were serious rivals of the adult players. The law students at the various "Inns" also had their plays, as did the students at Oxford and Cambridge—although the latter usually performed Latin and Greek plays, either in the original or in translation.

### THE PLAYERS

By Shakespeare's day acting had become a profession, but it was organised somewhat differently from the acting profession of today. A band of men and boys—women not being allowed to act in stage plays—would get together and apply to some well-known figure in public life for his patronage. If he thought them good enough he would adopt them and they would henceforth be known as The Earl of Pembroke's Men, The Lord Chamberlain's Company, The Admiral's Men, and so on. (Shakespeare himself was a member of the Lord Chamberlain's company, afterwards known as The King's Men.) The patron got nothing out of it except the distinction of having his own Company and presumably directing them to put on any particular play he wished and to perform at his own house when he was entertaining.

### THE ELIZABETHAN THEATRE

Until 1576 there was no theatre in England, although there were a number of these Companies. They acted in private houses or in public Halls; if they were favoured by a Royal Command they acted in one of the royal palaces. They spent much of their time "on tour" and in country towns or big villages they would put on a performance wherever they could erect a stage and leave room for an audience. Very often this was in the yard of the local inn, which usually had a balcony running around three sides on to which the guests' rooms opened and where spectators could sit or stand and look down at the play.

When the first theatre was built in London it naturally adopted many of the features of the places where performances had proved to be most successful—the great Halls (like those of the Colleges and the Inns of Court) and the inn-yards. In both, the audience came round three sides of the stage; in the inn-yard there was the balcony on three sides, but that

*See *The Theatre* by H. & R. Leacroft.

part of it which was directly above the stage would be curtained off and become a sort of upper stage from which actors could address their colleagues in the play below them, and in which characters could appear to the audience, but not to the players on the stage, and so over-hear what was going on without being observed. In both the inn-yard and the great Hall, also, there were doors *behind* the stage for the actors' entrances and exits.

### EFFECT OF THE THEATRE ON PLAYS

These factors, then, controlled the shape of the theatre which, with minor alterations, was in use during Shake-speare's day. It had its effect on his plays. Many a scene which seems absurd to us today was made much more credible when a character who was supposed to be neither seen nor heard by those on the stage was stationed on the balcony, per-haps peering round a curtain; and Shake-speare often made good use of the balcony in other ways, as when Juliet speaks to Romeo in the garden below her window—in fact the stage direction, "Enter so-and-so, *above*," occurs frequently and tells its own tale.

The fact that the stage jutted out into what we now call the auditorium also had its uses. We sometimes think the long solo speeches called "soliloquies" in Shakespeare's plays are unnatural; they hold up the action, for one thing, and in any case, who ever heard of a man talking aloud to himself at such length? But the soliloquies in Shakespeare's day were the high-lights. They usually contained fine poetic or dramatic lines and the actor would come to the very front of the stage,

6

*A drawing of the Swan Theatre made by Arend van Buchell from the instructions of Johannes de Witt, about* 1596

with no roof over their heads, incidentally —and they seem to agree on one thing: they were a noisy, disorderly crowd, eating apples, shouting, fighting, flirting and generally making a nuisance of themselves if something was not to their liking. It is a sobering thought that this rabble would keep silence to hear their favourites deliver a long and often difficult speech and break into genuine applause when it was over. What would be the reactions of a similar crowd to a poetic soliloquy in London or New York today?

This nearness of the audience—some of whom paid good money to sit actually *on* the stage—had other noticeable effects. A very popular device in Elizabethan drama was the "aside"—a short remark addressed to the audience and not intended to be heard by the other characters on the stage. In our modern theatres it strikes us as ridiculous and it has fortunately almost died out; but in Shakespeare's day it was eminently sensible; it was easy, when the audience was all round you and many of them only a few feet away from you, to throw a brief remark in their direction which they would hear, but not the other actors.

There was no stage lighting (and therefore no facial make-up) because performances were given only in daylight, but there was some dressing-up. Since all the female parts were played by boys or men the idea of special costumes was familiar to actors and audiences, but how far Romans were dressed as Romans, ancient Britons as ancient Britons, and so on, or whether most of the parts were played in Elizabethan dress, we cannot now say for certain. But we do know that

right among the audience, to deliver them. The public had its favourites then, as now, and when one of their "stars" came forward to declaim "All the world's a stage", or "To be, or not to be", or another of the great soliloquies, there would be a hushed silence until he had finished. Then he would bow and return to the centre of the stage to continue the play (or walk off if it was the end of a scene) unless he was recalled to give an encore! There are several accounts of the "groundlings"—the audience sitting or standing on the ground in the theatre,

7

properties were used because some of the original lists have survived; they include helmets, clubs, a lion's skin, a bear's skin, "Cerberus' three heads," and so on.

Of scenery there was very little—certainly nothing like the elaborate representations of forest glades, battlements, churches, and the like which we use today. The lists referred to above include a bedstead, a tree of golden apples, a little altar, "the City of Rome", "the cloth of the Sun and Moon" and "1 Hell mouth", so there was obviously some attempt to represent, or at least to suggest, different scenes. But for the most part it was left to the author to tell the audience all they wanted to know about the scene in the course of the play, helped out possibly by a board displayed every now and then with the necessary information. As the plays were acted in broad daylight it was particularly necessary to make it clear as soon as possible if a scene was supposed to be played at night, and lines like "'Tis now the witching hour of night"—or more poetical words to the same effect—occur frequently in all the plays of the time. One can only marvel at the power of the dramatist, and at the willingness of the Elizabethan audience to be deceived, when one realises that when, say, Lady Macbeth appeared in her night-dress, carrying a candle, the whole audience were prepared to accept the fact that on the stage it was midnight, although they could see the blue sky overhead and feel the sun beating down into the open pit!*

We are accustomed to seeing Shakespeare's plays cut up into separate scenes, some of them very short; in many modern productions a curtain will fall for a change of scene ten or a dozen times in the course of the play. But Shakespeare himself knew nothing of such divisions. In the earliest editions of his plays there are divisions into acts but not into scenes; these latter divisions were the work of later editors. Scene would flow into scene with scarcely a break, the actors walking off one side of the stage at the end of one and other actors entering at the other side, or by a different door, to signify the beginning of the next. Often, at the end of a scene in a Shakespeare play, you will notice two lines in rhyme, although the rest of the play is in blank verse. Whether this was a signal to the actors waiting to come on (and unable to see the stage) that the scene was about to finish, we cannot be certain, but it must have had some such purpose.

*There was one "indoor" theatre in Shakespeare's day which was used in the winter with some kind of artificial lighting by torches, but this was exceptional.

# II. The Man

Stratford-upon-Avon, where Shakespeare was born in 1564, was then a small town of about 2,000 people, who had reason to be proud of their glorious church, their splendid bridge over the river, their grammar school, and their ancient market and fairs.

The town's affairs were managed by a Corporation which, like the governing bodies of other towns and cities, had surprisingly wide powers. The Elizabethan Corporation could, and did, fix the prices of some commodities, punish idle apprentices, impound stray pigs and fine their owners, arrest and fine drunkards and runaway servants, and even do its best to make people go to church regularly. There are many references in Shakespeare's plays to "petty tyrants", Jacks-in-office, men "drest in a little brief authority," and so on, and these references would be highly appreciated by audiences who had reason to resent the activities of some officious local alderman or councillor.

Stratford was still, of course, primarily a *country* town; the fields and commons and private parks came close to its streets and Shakespeare was more a country boy than a town boy. The Warwickshire countryside is not dramatic; there are no mountains or bare uplands or deep valleys. Its beauty is quietly pastoral—quietly monotonous, perhaps, to visitors from lands of more vivid contrasts. But it finds its variety in the seasons' changes; spring-time and harvest, high summer and wintry blast—these provide its contrasts today as they did in the sixteenth century; and this is the country so easily and naturally reflected in Shakespeare's writing. You will seldom find descriptions of scenery in Shakespeare; the scenery is *there*, part of the established order of things, a pervading, subtle and inevitable background; and whether it is called Greece, Bohemia, Illyria, the Forest of Arden, or anything else, it is nearly always Warwickshire.

*Stratford-upon-Avon*

### SHAKESPEARE'S FAMILY

John Shakespeare, William's father, was a product of the Warwickshire countryside who had settled in Stratford and who made a living buying the wool and meat, the corn and leather from the

9

*Shakespeare's birthplace (restored)*

neighbouring farms and selling it to the townsfolk. It must have been a fairly prosperous trade, at any rate for some years, since he bought and rented property in Stratford and in due course became a member, an alderman, Chamberlain (*i.e.*, treasurer) and ultimately High Bailiff (*i.e.*, mayor) of the corporation which, fifteen years earlier, had fined him for allowing a muck-heap to accumulate outside his house.

His wife, Mary Arden, came of a good family and inherited a little property. She had eight children, of whom William was the third (his two older sisters died in infancy).

John Shakespeare's prosperity was short-lived. Ten years after his election as High Bailiff he was in debt and was forced to mortgage his wife's property. This was in 1578, when William was fourteen. We know little of his fortune for the next twenty years but by 1597 William had achieved considerable fame and success and was buying property in Stratford. In 1599 John made a second application for the grant of a coat-of-arms, which was successful, and it is pleasant to think that the son helped in this and other ways to brighten his father's last years. John Shakespeare died in 1601.

### BOYHOOD AND YOUTH

Everything we "know" about Shakespeare's boyhood is guesswork and legend. We do not even know the exact date of his birth nor whether he went to school. It is possible that he was born on April 22nd (1564—we do know the year) and it is probable that he went to the free Grammar School in Stratford; but there are no documents of any kind which give us precise and authoritative information about him between his baptism in 1564 and his marriage in 1582. By way of compensation we have various legends and traditions to fall back on, and there are a number of conclusions, or inspired guesses, which seem to be justified by the facts and which help to build up a reasonably full picture.

Let us look at the conclusions and guesses first. As the son of a prominent citizen William would surely go to school (although schooling was not compulsory). As there was (and still is) a flourishing Grammar School in Stratford, it is at least probable that William would attend it. It was a good school for its time— or it ought to have been, seeing that the schoolmaster's salary was double that paid to the Master at Eton. Shakespeare's references to schoolboys and masters in his works are frequent enough, but they suggest that he was never an enthusiastic pupil and retained few kind or sympathetic memories of his masters. If our modern experience is anything to go by, this suggests that he left school early, since few boys really come to appreciate either their teachers or their studies until they are 16 or 17. In 1578, when William was fourteen, his father was in the midst of his financial troubles; it would not be surprising if he found it necessary then, or soon afterwards, to take his oldest boy away from school to help him in his business.

What would he have learnt in the four or five years at the Grammar School? To read, certainly. To write? Yes, and we must beware of thinking in terms of our own day. If you look at the few samples of Shakespeare's handwriting that have survived you will begin to doubt whether he ever did learn to write; yet that tortured, squiggly script was the accepted handwriting of his day and we can only assume that, through constant practice, he and his contemporaries found it easier to read than we do.

But apart from reading and writing it is difficult to be certain what was taught in the Elizabethan Grammar Schools. We know that Shakespeare knew some Latin, although he used translations so freely that he could have managed with very little. There is no evidence that he knew any Greek. Presumably he learnt to "reckon", but again there is no proof. In fact the sixteenth-century school curriculum remains something of a mystery. Perhaps his life-long dislike of schooling arose as much from memories of complete boredom as from the normal healthy aversion to discipline!

Another important conclusion may be drawn from the recorded fact that John

*'Shakespeare's classroom', the Grammar School, Stratford-upon-Avon, as it was early in the present century*

Shakespeare, while High Bailiff, secured the Earl of Leicester's Players to perform plays in Stratford on several occasions. That shows, at least, that he was interested in play-acting, since it was not every Corporation that provided these entertainments—which had to be paid for out of the town's exchequer. Even if they were private performances for the "Mayor and Corporation and friends" it is at least likely that John would take his oldest son to see them. In addition to these formal occasions there were almost certainly frequent visits of other travelling bands of actors, some of them less respectable, no doubt, than the Earl of Leicester's men. The young Shakespeare must have seen more plays performed by actors on the stage than the great majority of boys in any provincial town in Europe or America sees in the twentieth century.

The legends and traditions are naturally numerous; when a man becomes famous there are always people who "remember" incidents connected with his youth. Some of these memories are genuine; others owe more to the narrator's imagination than to the truth. One story tells how the youthful Shakespeare would sometimes kill a calf for his father and improve the occasion with an exhibition of dramatic oratory—whether of his own (which would anticipate the poet in him) or from some stage play (which would suggest the future actor) is not disclosed. Another tradition says that he was an usher (*i.e.*, an assistant master) at a country school, a post for which he could have had little inclination and even less qualification. As we shall presently see, these legends were but the precursors of many others.

The next thing we know for certain was that in 1582 the Bishop of Worcester (in whose diocese Stratford was then situated) issued a licence for the marriage of William Shakespeare and Anne Hathaway. No record has been found of the actual marriage and we do not know where it took place. Shakespeare, it will be noted, was eighteen; from the age of his wife, given on her tombstone, we can calculate that she was twenty-six at the time of her marriage. For a boy of eighteen to marry a woman of twenty-six is generally supposed to be ominous; and did not Shakespeare himself say (or make one of his characters say) in *Twelfth Night:*

> Let still the woman take
> An elder than herself; so wears she
> to him,
> So sways she level in her husband's
> heart . . . . ?

The fact is, we do not know whether this was or was not a happy marriage; as we shall see, Will was away from home for long spells and did not return to settle in Stratford until about 1611—and the general opinion is that absence makes the heart grow fonder. In any case he did return.

William and Anne had three children. Susanna, born in 1583, married Dr Hall of Stratford and died at the age of 66; Judith, born in 1585, married Thomas Quiney, vintner, of Stratford and died in 1662 at the age of 77 (a ripe old age for the Shakespeare family); and Hamnet, twin brother of Judith, died at the age of eleven. Susanna had a daughter and Judith had three children, but none of Shakespeare's grandchildren produced a

*Charlecote, a typical Elizabethan manor house*

family and there were no descendants living after 1670.

### THE "LOST YEARS"

With the year 1586 we return to legends and traditions. In that year he is said to have been "unlucky" in a poaching exploit on the land of Sir Thomas Lucy of Charlecote Park (adjoining Stratford). There is more solid foundation than usual for this legend, but still no proof. It is often assumed that this was a boyish escapade, but Shakespeare in 1586 was a married man of twenty-two, with three children. If he really was in the habit of poaching deer at that age it looks as though the stern necessity of making both ends meet was a more likely motive than youthful irresponsibility. He is said to have aggravated his offence by writing rude rhymes about Sir Thomas Lucy, making Stratford so hot for himself that he ran away to London.

We know nothing more of his activities until 1593, so that, from his marriage in 1582, there is a period of eleven years for which there is literally no evidence, no firm biographical facts whatever apart from the conjectured poaching incident and the recorded baptism of his three children. They are the "lost years."*

Legend and tradition have naturally been busy, and some of the legends are quite well authenticated. Some say he held the horses of gallants while they were in the theatre; others that he joined a company of actors who happened to visit Stratford and remained with them until they reached London, when he became a member of a more reputable company. Some make him a lawyer's clerk, some a soldier, some a tutor in a noble family in the north of England or in Gloucestershire. All that we know for certain is that by 1592 he had become known as a playwright, by 1593 as a poet and by 1594 as an actor.

The evidence for his reputation as a playwright occurs in an outburst of jealous resentment by Robert Greene, another playwright, who refers bitterly to the activities of one whom he calls "Shake-scene" and who, from other hints and side-kicks, we can only assume to have been Shakespeare. The evidence for the poetic reputation is direct, unmistakable, and in black and white.

*They were eventful years in British history, including as they did the execution of Mary, Queen of Scots, Drake's expedition to Cartagena and Cadiz, the defeat of the Spanish Armada, and Sir Richard Grenville's fight in the *Revenge.*

13

In April, 1593, Richard Field—a printer who came from Stratford-upon-Avon—published *Venus and Adonis*, a poem of nearly two hundred six-line stanzas, dedicated to the Earl of Southampton by William Shakespeare. Most of the poem is a description of the temptation of Adonis by Venus, and by our modern standards it is tedious and highly-coloured. But it was immensely popular in its day, and the fact that it was dedicated to a young nobleman who at that time enjoyed the Queen's favour shows that the poet, if he really came to London, an unknown country youth, in 1586, had reached the highest circles of London "society" in the remarkably short period of seven years.

In the next year Richard Field published *Lucrece*, a second poem by the same poet, dedicated to the same noble Lord. It is in 265 stanzas of seven lines each. The story—which was already familiar in its broad outlines to most of his readers—might have been made into a great tragedy if Shakespeare had brooded on it for a few more years, and although it was well received it had not the same success as *Venus and Adonis*.

Besides these two long poems other collections of Shakespeare's verses were published later, in 1609, although most of them were probably written by 1594, and a volume of verses attributed to Shakespeare but mostly the work of others was published in 1599. The best

*Shakespeare's rise to fame illustrated in the title pages of the first quartos of his plays; note the dates and the increasing prominence of the playwright's name*

and most famous of these collections is undoubtedly the *Sonnets*.

While the other poems of Shakespeare are very much the product of his age, being the re-telling of popular legends in

M. William Shak-ſpeare:

*HIS*

True Chronicle Hiſtorie of the life and death of King L E A R and his three Daughters.

*With the vnfortunate life of* Edgar, *ſonne* and heire to the Earle of Gloſter, and his ſullen and aſſumed humor of T O M of Bedlam :

*As it was played before the Kings Maieſtie at Whitehall vpon S. Stephans night in Chriſtmas Hollidayes.*

By his Maieſties ſeruants playing vſually at the Gloabe on the Bancke-ſide.

L O N D O N,
Printed for *Nathaniel Butter*, and are to be ſold at his ſhop in *Pauls* Church-yard at the ſigne of the Pide Bull neere S'. *Auſtins* Gate. 1 6 0 8

# The moſt excellent

Hiſtorie of the *Merchant of Venice*.

VVith the extreame crueltie of *Shylocke* the Iewe towards the ſayd Merchant, in cutting a iuſt pound of his fleſh : and the obtayning of *Portia* by the choyſe of three cheſts.

*As it hath beene diuers times acted by the Lord Chamberlaine his Seruants.*

Written by William Shakeſpeare.

AT LONDON,
Printed by *I. R.* for Thomas Heyes,
and are to be ſold in Paules Church-yard, at the ſigne of the Greene Dragon.
1 6 0 0

highly-figurative, highly-polished Elizabethan verse, the Sonnets are more universal in their interest and in their style. Most of them, however, are subtle and reflective and the complete understanding of them taxes even the adult mind. The "story" behind the Sonnets, if there is one, is one of the unsolved mysteries of Shakespeare's life and work.

### SHAKESPEARE THE ACTOR

There are various traditions pointing to Shakespeare's enrolment in one or other of the Companies of Players soon after his arrival in London, but we do not

depend entirely on tradition. The official records of the Lord Chamberlain (the Queen's Treasurer) show that as early as 1594 he was directed—together with two famous actors, Kempe and Burbage—to present two comedies before the Queen at Greenwich Palace in December of that year; this means that by 1594 Shakespeare was not only an accepted poet and a reputable actor but that he must have held some position of seniority in the Lord Chamberlain's Company (otherwise he would not have been mentioned by name). The *Plays* of Ben Jonson, published in 1598, also contains a list of the chief actors, including Shakespeare. The idea that acting was a secondary interest, which he rejected when he had become famous as a playwright, is dispelled by the appearance of his name in the list of actors in Jonson's was right displeasant to him and his people, as shoulde appeare in that it was a custome many yeares after, that no Knightes were made in Norway, excepte they were first sworne to reuenge the slaughter of theyr countreymen and frendes thus slayne in Scotland.

*The othe that knightes tooke in Norway, to reuenge the death of theyr frendes.*

The Scottes hauing wonne so notable a victory, after they had gathered and diuided the spoyle of the fielde, caused solemne processions to be made in all places of the realme, and thankes to be giuen to almightie God, that had sent them so fayre a day ouer their enimies.

*Solemne processions for victory gotté.*

But whylest the people were thus at theyr processions, worde was brought that a newe fleete of Danes was arriued at Kingcorne, sent thither by Canute king of England in renenge of his brothers Suenos ouerthrow.

*A power of Danes arriued at Kyncorne out of Englã d.*

To resist these enimies, whiche were already landed, and busie in spoiling the countrey, Makbeth and Banquho were sente with the kings authoritie, who hauing with them a conuenient power, encountred the enimies, siewe parte of them, and chased the other to their shippes. They that escaped, and got once to theyr shippes, obtayned of Makbeth for a great summe of golde, that suche of theyr freendes as were slaine at this last bickering might be buried in Saint Colmes Inche. In memorie whereof, many olde Sepultures are yet in the sayde Inche, there to be seene grauen with the armes of the Danes, as

*The Danes vanquished by Makbeth and Banquho.*

*Danes buried in S. Colmes Inche.*

the maner of burying noble men still is, and heretofore hath bene vsed.

A peace was also concluded at the same time betwixte the Danes and Scottishmen, ratified as some haue wrytten in this wise. That from thence foorth the Danes shoulde neuer come into Scotlande to make any warres agaynst the Scottes by any maner of meanes.

*A peace concluded betwixt Scottes and Danes.*

And these were the warres that Duncane had with forrayne enimies in the seuenth yeare of his reygne.

Shortly after happened a straunge and vncouth wonder, whiche afterwarde was the cause of muche trouble in the realme of Scotlande as ye shall after heare. It fortuned as Makbeth & Banquho iourneyed towarde Fores, where the king as then lay, they went sporting by the way togither without other companie, saue only themselues, passing through the woodes and fieldes, when sodenly in the middes of a launde, there met them .iij. women in straunge & ferly apparell, resembling creatures of an elder worlde, whom when they attentiuely beheide, wondering much at the sight, The first of them spake & sayde: All hayle Makbeth Thane of Glammis (for he had lately entred into that dignitie and office by the death of his father Synel.) The .ij. of them said: Hayle Makbeth Thane of Cawder: but the third sayde: All hayle Makbeth that hereafter shall be king of Scotland.

*The prophesie of three wom= supposing to be the weird si= sters or feiries.*

Then Banquho, what maner of women (saith he) are you, that seeme so little fauourable vnto me, where as to my fellow here, besides highe offices, yee assigne also the kingdome, appointyng foorth nothing for me at all? Yes sayth the firste of them, wee promise greater benefites vnto thee, than vnto him, for he shall reygne in deede, but with an vnluckie ende: neyther shall he leaue any issue behinde him to succeede

in his place, where contrarily thou in deede shalt not reygne at all, but of thee those shall be borne whiche shall gouerne the Scottishe kingdome by long order of continuall discent. Herewith the foresayde women vanished immediatly out of theyr sight . This was reputed at the first but some vayne fantasticall illusion by Makbeth and Banquho, in so muche that Banquho woulde call Makbeth in ieste kyng of Scot-

*A thing to wooden at.*

Q.ij.

*Macbeth and the Witches: a page from Holinshed's 'Chronicles' (British Museum) one of Shakespeare's source-books. (Compare pp. 45–46)*

*Sejanus* in 1603, while in the same year he was mentioned among the actors licensed by James I on his accession (the Lord Chamberlain's Company by this time having become the King's Men). In addition to these mentions and the different traditions there are the innumerable references to the stage and to acting which occur all through the Plays and which suggest that their author was at least familiar with the actor's life and the pleasures and pains of his profession—so familiar, indeed, that we are justified in accepting the fact that he must have spent many years treading the boards.

### FIRST PLAYS

We can only guess the steps by which the raw young man from Stratford rose in a few years to be a competent actor (it is generally agreed on good authority that he never played "the lead" and that "the top of his performance" was the part of the ghost in *Hamlet*), a prosperous part-owner of a flourishing Company of Players, a successful poet and an outstanding dramatist. But we can be fairly confident about one of the stages through which he passed—the apprentice playwright. In the three years, 1590 to 1592, he wrote three comedies, *Love's Labour's Lost*, *The Comedy of Errors* and *Two Gentlemen of Verona* (the last two of which were popular successes) and "touched up" a gruesome tragedy, *Titus Andronicus*, and the three Parts of *Henry VI*. The job of improving or partly rewriting old plays—and new ones, too, for that matter—would naturally be given to a member of the Company who was known to have a ready pen and there are several other plays of the period in which some scholars have detected the hand of Shakespeare. A young man who is keen to become a writer of plays attaches great importance to his first *produced* work, and although we do not today think very highly of these early plays compared with those that came after, we may be sure that Shakespeare was only too happy to see them acted and no less eager to take on the refurbishing of the work of other hands.

### CONTEMPORARY TRIBUTES

It is to this refurbishing that we owe the earliest reference to Shakespeare the playwright—the outburst of the aggrieved rival, Greene. He referred to "an upstart crow, beautified with our feathers"—a clear indication that Greene's plays were among those rewritten by "Shake-scene". This was in 1592 and later in the same year the attack was answered by another contemporary playwright, who may also have "suffered" refurbishing but who spoke up generously for the upstart crow. In 1598 a country clergyman named Francis Meres published a book in which he referred to the "honey-tongued Shakespeare" as being famous for his *Venus and Adonis*, his *Lucrece* and "his sugared sonnets among his private friends." He goes on to mention his plays, naming all those attributed to Shakespeare by this date except the three *Henry VI* plays. Later references are frequent but are less important, since by 1599 Shakespeare was so well known and so highly esteemed that the publishers of his works printed his name prominently on the title-page—by no means a regular practice at that time.

## "BACONIAN" AND OTHER THEORIES OF AUTHORSHIP

The comparative scarcity of thoroughly reliable contemporary evidence about Shakespeare, combined with the apparent contrast between his humble birth and education on the one hand, and his amazing brilliance and all-round knowledge on the other, have led many people to suspect that the works of Shakespeare as we know them were not written by the man Shakespeare of Stratford to whom they are attributed. The chief claimant for the honour of their authorship is Sir Francis Bacon, and the so-called Baconian Theory has had many followers for over a century. There is, indeed, a whole library of books on the theory, some reasonable and well-balanced, others more than a little mad.

Others have put forward the Earl of Oxford, the Earl of Derby, Sir Edward Dyer, and even a kind of syndicate of authors as the genuine author of Shakespeare's plays. As recently as 1955 an American professor published a reasoned case for the authorship of most of Shakespeare's plays by Christopher Marlowe, a brilliant young poet and dramatist who is generally believed to have been killed in a fight in 1593 at the age of twenty-nine.

It would be absurd to dismiss these ideas as nonsense when scholars have spent many years in propounding or supporting them.

Only by matching scholarship with scholarship can we refute the various theories. As ordinary admirers of "Shakespeare" we have two alternatives. We can argue that the Shakespeare we accept was only a man, albeit an extraordinary man. He obviously had a remarkable gift for extracting information from books and people—especially from people— and reproducing it with all the confidence of first-hand experience. Of course he was a genius; but the emergence of a genius at any time or in any country is by no means rare. The point is that there is nothing we know about Shakespeare or his work which cannot be explained by the mere statement that he was a genius.

That is one attitude we can adopt. The other is simpler—and perhaps lazier. We can decline to worry about *who* wrote Shakespeare's plays; for all we care it could have been, if not Shakespeare, somebody else of the same name! What we are interested in—and it is a large enough interest for one person's lifetime —is the body of plays and poems we know as William Shakespeare's.

## A MAN OF PROPERTY

To return to the life of Shakespeare, we find every indication that he prospered financially from about 1596 onwards, and that he drove a hard bargain and invested his money carefully. As Mr Ivor Brown has written, "Antony might hurl away an Empire; his creator went out and bought another acre."

His income was derived from three main sources. The least profitable would be the publication of his plays and poems. Managers paid outright for a play (usually about £10 to a well-established author) although they might add a bonus or even a share of the profits if the play was highly successful. Even two plays a year would not have brought Shakespeare a fortune.

Next came his pay as an actor. In a

*The Globe*

*The Globe Theatre, Bankside, from Visscher's View of London, 1616*

first-rate Company an actor might easily earn £250 or £300 a year and even if he acted only occasionally, in minor parts, Shakespeare must have earned between £100 and £200 a year for some years.

But his most fruitful source of income was his part ownership of theatres. In 1599 he became a sharer in the profits of the Globe Theatre and in 1610 he began to draw a share of the profits of the Blackfriars Theatre. We do not know how many shares he held in these ventures—which must have cost him money in the first place, of course—but his income from all sources was probably not less than £500 a year at first, rising to £800 or more after 1610. In terms of modern purchasing power this would represent an income of several thousand

pounds a year. The small-town boy had indeed made good!

If he was prosperous, however, he was also extremely busy. One can only marvel at the industry and speed of the man who could write one, two or even three full-length plays in a year, attend the rehearsals, assist in the management of the theatre, touch up or re-write plays, or parts of plays, when necessary, and be prepared to act in plays other than his own when required. It is significant that one of his poems, *Venus and Adonis*, and part of another, *Lucrece*, were written in 1593, a year when the theatre was closed for months because of an outbreak of the plague.

He spent most of his money on property, mainly in his home town. In 1597 he bought the best house in the town, New Place, for £60—a price which, even allowing for the change in money value, suggests that it might have been somewhat dilapidated. From then onwards we have records of other purchases, some running into hundreds of pounds, some almost trifling; the final result was that when he finally retired to Stratford it was as a man of means—not wealthy, perhaps, but certainly very "warm".

### HIS GREATEST PERIOD

For about ten years, from 1600 to 1610, Shakespeare remained on the heights. They were heights, moreover, which have seldom been attained by any other writer and certainly never held for so long. During that period he passed from perfect romantic comedy to the depths of tragic intensity, but whether he was writing love-scenes in the Forest of Arden or portraying the mental agonies of a Hamlet or an Othello, his powers of invention and imagination, his human sympathy and understanding, and his command of beautiful, closely-packed language never failed him.

We shall be considering separately the plays of this period, but it is as a group that they need to be envisaged if we are to begin to appreciate the miracle. Other dramatists have written an isolated play which can bear comparison with an isolated play from this period of Shakespeare's maturity; some have written more than one; but for one man to have written, in the space of ten years, *As You Like It, Twelfth Night, Hamlet, Othello, King Lear, Macbeth, Antony and Cleopatra*, and *Coriolanus*, besides three or four less majestic plays (which would have been considered outstanding at any other period), is almost miraculous. When it is remembered that for part of the period he was acting in some of his own and others' plays and helping to run the affairs of a successful theatre (which involved "editing" inferior work by older dramatists) and living the crowded life of a popular and successful business man in London, the miracle passes ordinary comprehension. There are no standards by which we can measure this man.

*The monument in Stratford Church*

### HIS WITHDRAWAL TO STRATFORD

We do not know for certain when Shakespeare "retired" but at this point in his career a little intelligent guess-work is justified. We know that he had a comfortable house to go home to; we know that he had a comfortable income; his older daughter made a good marriage in 1607 and he was a grandfather by the end of that year. He had every reason to contemplate retiring from the exhausting life he had been leading and he must have dreaded the fate that so often awaits the successful author. If neglect and displacement by a rising generation were to be his lot—as they might well be if his powers began to fail—he would be well advised to retire at the height of his fame.

And that, approximately, is what he did. After his "greatest period" he wrote

20

only two or three plays. In the last of them, *The Tempest*, he wrote his farewell to the theatre, as we shall see. That was in 1611, which is the year usually accepted by scholars for his withdrawal to Stratford. It is reasonable to suppose that he had paid more frequent visits home during the few years before, and that he paid occasional visits to London in the few years after his retirement, but there is no certain evidence on these points.

### HIS DEATH

He did not enjoy his retirement for long. His was not a long-lived family, and he may have over-strained a not very robust constitution; whatever the reason, he was only 52 when he died.

The burial register at the church records simply, under the date April 25th (1616), "Will. Shakespeare, gent." and neither the owlish and unworthy portrait bust on his monument in the parish church, nor the doggerel verses on his grave, tell us any more than that about one of the greatest men of all time.

His wife outlived him by seven years.

# III. The Comedies

### SOURCES

We have to remind ourselves every now and then that the plots of Shakespeare's plays were the only part of them which was not original. That seems rather startling at first. Surely, one of the attractions of a play is seeing how it ends —which boy gets which girl, or, if it is a mystery-thriller, "who done it". But is that such a great attraction after all? If it were so very important nobody would ever wish to see a play twice, yet people go again and again to see a good play. It begins to look as though the plot is not so important after all.

Obviously it was not so important to Elizabethan audiences. There were no doubt some among the "groundlings" who were not great readers and who did not know the stories of Shakespeare's plays; but the majority would have read or heard the story in some form or another. What they came to the theatre for was to see how the author had handled the familiar story, whether he had improved on it, what new characters he had introduced, how he had got round this or that particular difficulty. Others would come to see their favourite actors either in a new part or in some well-loved familiar role—just as we play over and over some gramophone record we are particularly fond of. Others again were captured by the magic of the poetry, in a Shakespeare play especially. The *last* thing the audience expected to see was some surprising new story.

So Shakespeare used stories with which his audiences would already be familiar, at least in a general way. That he improved upon them goes without saying. He would twist the story round to make it more dramatic, inventing new characters, filling out small parts, introducing incidents from other stories, and so on. And of course he would fling over it all the magic cloak of his brilliant dialogue so that even those most familiar with the outlines of his story might find it difficult to recognise them.

### THREE EARLY COMEDIES

*Love's Labour's Lost* was one of Shakespeare's first plays, if not actually the first—and he seems for once to have made up the plot himself. Not that there is much plot. The King of Navarre and three of his courtiers have sworn to study for three years—and their oath prevents them from having any speech or contact with women. But the Princess of France comes with her ladies to discuss state affairs, whereupon the King of Navarre falls in love with her, and his three courtiers with three of the ladies in the Princess's train.

After centuries of neglect this play was brought back to the English stage after the 1939–45 war and proved unexpectedly popular. It was not the plot that made it a success, however, but the clever staging, the poetry, the bright kaleidoscope of the dresses and, perhaps most of all, the fun of the sub-plot, at times solemn, at other times high-spirited.

*Two Gentlemen of Verona* and *The Comedy of Errors* are two other early comedies which Shakespeare wrote between 1591 and 1592. They are both plays of intrigue and disguise, both highly entertaining (especially the latter), but both the sort of play that any playwright worth his salt could have turned out at the time for the convenience of the manager and the enjoyment of the public. They have their bright Shakespearean mo-

ments, it is true, but only an occasional speech and one or two original comic characters give any hint of what is to come. *Love's Labour's Lost*, for all its feeble story and its artificial love-making, is the most "Shakespearean" of these three plays.

### A MIDSUMMER NIGHT'S DREAM

The love-making in this play is still artificial, but the play itself is a great advance on the earlier comedies. Two lovers, Hermia and Lysander, are not allowed to marry and they wander away from Athens into the country. Another young man, Demetrius, is in love with Hermia (who can see nothing in him) and follows her and Lysander. Demetrius in his turn is followed by Helena, who is madly in love with him although he, Demetrius, has no use for Helena. The four of them stray into the part of the woods ruled by the fairies, where King Oberon is anxious to teach Queen Titania a lesson. He orders Puck to find the juice of a plant which, when squeezed on her eyelids, will make her fall in love

OBERON: *Fetch me that flow'r, the herb I showed thee once.* (*A Midsummer Night's Dream*, II, i, 169)

TITANIA: *Sleep thou, and I will wind thee in my arms.* (*A Midsummer Night's Dream IV, i,* 45)

with the first thing she sees when she awakes.

In the woods some villagers are rehearsing a play to perform before Duke Theseus at his wedding and Puck, coming upon them at their rehearsal, casts a magic spell on Bottom, one of the actors, which turns his head into that of an ass. Bottom, complete with ass's head, is the first thing Titania sees when she wakes up and she begins to make a fuss of him.

Puck squeezes the magic juice on Lysander's eyes (mistaking him for Demetrius) and as Helena is the first person he sees on waking he (Lysander) makes love to her. Oberon tries to correct Puck's mistake by anointing Demetrius's eyes while he sleeps, but unfortunately Helena is the first person *he* sees when he wakes up. So Lysander and Demetrius go off to fight a duel over Helena, while

Helena and Hermia also quarrel bitterly. But Oberon puts everything right at the end and the play finishes with the comical production of the play by Bottom and his friends.

Of all Shakespeare's plays this is perhaps the best constructed, although it is one of the earliest. Modern producers sometimes omit a scene here and there from a Shakespeare play; or they change the order of the scenes, or run two or three together. With "The Dream" (as it is affectionately known by theatre people) it would be impossible to omit a scene without losing something essential, while to change the scenes about would only spoil the existing smooth arrangement.

The scene is set in "Athens, and a wood near it" but a great deal of the play is very typically English and there are references to English scenes and people—including the Queen. Puck, a spirit, talks to Oberon, a fairy, standing in a wood in ancient Greece, about "russet-pated choughs" rising and cawing "at the gun's report"—although choughs are English birds and there were no guns in ancient Greece; and the play-acting and rehearsing of the "rude mechanicals" is in the best tradition of English broad farce. And what could be more English than Oberon's description of the place where Titania sleeps?

> I know a bank where the wild thyme
> blows,
> Where oxlips and the nodding violet
> grows;
> Quite over-canopied with luscious
> woodbine,
> With sweet musk-roses, and with
> eglantine.

## THE MERCHANT OF VENICE

There are two distinct stories in this play but they are so skilfully interwoven that they seem like one.

Bassanio is anxious to go to Belmont to try to win the hand of Portia, so he asks his friend Antonio, a Venetian merchant, to lend him some money. Antonio is short of ready cash, as his ships are still at sea, so he borrows from Shylock, who lends him the necessary amount on condition that if he does not pay up by the agreed date he will pay Shylock with a pound of his flesh.

Portia's father has made an absurd arrangement to prevent her from choosing a husband rashly. Her suitors have to guess which of the three caskets, one gold, one silver and one lead, contains her portrait. Other suitors guess wrongly, but Bassanio is luckier and wins his Portia.

He learns, to his horror, that Antonio's ships have not come home, that he has failed to pay Shylock and has been cast into prison. Portia is struck by the depth of these men's friendship and sends Bassanio back in haste to Venice with enough money to pay the debt three times over; but Shylock refuses the money; he insists on his pound of flesh.

When the case is heard in court it looks as though Antonio is to lose—which means his death, since Shylock demands his pound of flesh cut from the heart. But an unknown young lawyer—who is Portia in disguise—turns the scales by declaring that if Shylock (who is sharpening his knife in anticipation) spills as much as one drop of Christian blood in cutting his pound of flesh, his life, by the law of Venice, will be forfeit. Shylock realises he is defeated and, after he has been fined

for endangering the life of a Christian, he slinks away, humiliated.

The play ends in laughter. Portia, in disguise, asks Bassanio (who has offered her anything she likes to ask for) to give her the ring he is wearing—which Portia had given him. He hesitates, but has to give it to the young judge. When he gets home without it, Portia, who has removed her disguise, is indignant and makes things uncomfortable for him for a while. There is a charming sub-plot about the love between Lorenzo and Jessica, the daughter of Shylock.

It is all nonsense, of course. No father would impose such a ridiculous "test" for his daughter's suitors; no money-lender would demand a pound of flesh for non-payment; the laws of Venice are fantastic; and it is absurd to imagine that Bassanio would not recognise Portia as the young advocate. But who cares? It

PORTIA: *Art thou contented, Jew?*
*What dost thou say?*
(*Merchant of Venice, IV, i,* 393)

makes a good play, which is what Shake-speare intended and his audience demanded. It also demanded a Jew for a villain as it was generally believed that the Queen's Jewish doctor, Lopez, had recently been plotting her death. Shakespeare no doubt meant to portray Shylock as the arch-villain—as indeed he did—but he could not prevent himself from creating Shylock as, at the same time, a human being. Whether Shylock should be played pathetically, inviting us to sympathise with him as the representative of a martyred and suffering race; or whether, like Gratiano in the play, we should rejoice in his downfall—these are questions which each must answer for himself.

### THE MERRY WIVES OF WINDSOR

Critics have always tended to sniff at this play. It is said to have been written in a fortnight in response to an expressed wish of the Queen to see "Sir John" (Falstaff) "in love"—she had already seen Sir John drunk and Sir John at war in the Henry IV plays which we shall consider presently. It is true that a royal command of this kind is no substitute for inspiration; it is also true that there is practically none of Shakespeare's poetry in it, and none of the characters reveals the depth of Shakespeare's human sympathy and understanding. But what a rip-roaring farce it is! If the Queen enjoyed it as much as modern audiences enjoy it, three-and-a-half centuries later, both she and Shakespeare must have been satisfied.

As it turned out, she did not after all see Sir John "in love". He makes love to Mistress Ford and Mistress Page for

*The merry wives of Windsor hide Falstaff in the dirty linen basket*

their money, and the merry wives make a fool of him. Mistress Ford's husband, needlessly jealous, almost catches him and he escapes only by being carried out in a basket of dirty linen and thrown into the river. He comes back a second time, however, and this time gets away disguised as an old woman and is thoroughly cudgelled by Ford as he makes his escape. He still believes that Mistress Ford loves him, however, and agrees to meet her at night in Windsor Forest, disguised as Herne the Hunter. A crowd of "fairies"—the local children—dance round him pinching him and scorching him with torches and in the general merriment the whole story comes out; he takes his humiliation in the right spirit and is forgiven. In the general merriment, also, "Sweet Anne Page", daughter of Mistress Page, is seized by the young man whom she loves but who is not her parents' choice for her—but these two are also forgiven.

There is a large company of minor parts and the play, besides being highly amusing for everybody except the highest-browed, is also one of the most English of all Shakespeare's plays.

### THE TAMING OF THE SHREW

This is another comedy written at about the same time; much of it is a re-hash of another play by an unknown author. It tells how the surly spit-fire Katharina, is tamed by Petruchio. She ends up his devoted and even servile wife, but the treatment has included a good deal of whip-cracking and some heartless practical jokes.

### MUCH ADO ABOUT NOTHING

This is the first of Shakespeare's "great" comedies. His period of great tragedies, from *Hamlet* to *Coriolanus*, lasted for about eight years, from 1602 to 1609; but the period of the great comedies was much shorter—in fact *Much Ado*, *As You Like It* and *Twelfth Night* were all written in the period 1599–1601.

All three of these plays have a serious element mingled with the comedy, and *Much Ado* is almost tragic at one point. It is mainly the story of Benedick and Beatrice—the former having vowed he would stay a bachelor and the latter having always despised men. They come together in the end because they are united over pity for Beatrice's cousin, Hero. She is about to marry Claudio, but an enemy of Claudio's stages a love scene at a window with another girl dressed in Hero's clothes. Claudio too readily believes what he thinks he sees and, at the church, he scornfully rejects the hand of Hero, who falls into a dead faint. The friar who was to have conducted the wedding persuades Hero's father, after the guests have de-

BEATRICE: *What fire is in my ears? Can this be true?* (*Much Ado, III, i,* 107)

parted thinking Hero dead, to pretend that she really *is* dead. Beatrice, who is convinced of her cousin's innocence, tells Benedick to "kill Claudio" if he really wants to prove himself and although Hero's innocence is proved before he has a chance to carry out Beatrice's command, his readiness to do so convinces her of his love. Claudio, who is deeply contrite when he hears how he was deceived—and who still thinks his rejection of Hero at the altar has caused her death—agrees to marry any bride whom Hero's family ask him to marry; they bring Hero, masked and veiled, and when she unveils and they are happily reunited, Benedick and Beatrice also "plight their troth".

Shakespeare's genius is noticeable in many different ways in this play. One of the master-strokes is in the way the "constable" (Dogberry) comes to Leonato, Hero's father, to report that the watch has taken a prisoner, but is so terribly longwinded that Leonato, who is actually on his way to Hero's wedding, has to get rid of Dogberry and tell him

26

to examine the prisoner himself. If Dogberry had come to the point quickly and said straight out what he had to say, Leonato himself would have seen the prisoner and discovered the plot in time. Another example of sustained genius is the battle of wits between Beatrice and Benedick. The quick-fire dialogue between these two can still keep an audience laughing, after so many years. So can the broader comedy of Dogberry and Verges.

### AS YOU LIKE IT

The serious element of this comedy is less pronounced than that of *Much Ado* and the gay and witty elements are even gayer and wittier. Rosalind, the heroine, is gentler than Beatrice, just as Orlando is more romantic than Benedick. Their cross-talk—Rosalind's and Orlando's—sparkles as much as Benedick's and Beatrice's, but it has a deeper tinge of romance, which makes it more tender and more moving. The play also has a far longer cast of interesting minor characters.

The story is one of Shakespeare's slightest. Orlando, a victim of family jealousy, wins a wrestling match at Duke Frederick's court and at the same time wins the love of Rosalind, who is the Duke's niece. Her father, the Duke Senior, is in exile, his estates having been usurped by Duke Frederick. When Frederick banishes Rosalind, his own daughter, Celia, will not be parted from her and, having collected Touchstone, the court Jester, they leave the court. Orlando—who has also been turned out of doors—comes across the banished Duke, who is kind to him.

In the forest Orlando meets Rosalind,

ROSALIND: *I could find it in my heart to disgrace my man's apparel, and to cry like a woman.* (*As You Like It*, II, iv, 4)

but does not recognise her as she is dressed as a man. (She and Celia have adopted false names and given out that they are brother and sister shepherds, although they do not appear to have any sheep!) Rosalind still loves Orlando but wishes to keep her disguise, so she encourages him to *pretend* that she is his Rosalind and offers to teach him how to love. He plays the game as well as he can but now and then finds it almost too much; Rosalind, for her part, is nearly at breaking point.

Orlando's wicked brother comes to the forest and is saved from death by Orlando. He is reconciled to Orlando, becomes a reformed character and falls in love with Celia. Duke Frederick is also converted and the exiled Duke is restored to his estates. Rosalind cunningly arranges a meeting at which she discloses her identity and all the lovers in the play are married.

This play, and possibly *Macbeth*, have more than any others been responsible for much of the murder of Shakespeare that has gone on for generations in the schoolrooms and examination halls. Other plays can stand a good deal of close study of notes, "sources", date of composition and so on. They are robust in their plots, they contain humour which has retained its freshness, characters and situations which never lose their attraction. But *As You Like It* is too frail a play for this sort of treatment. It is not even a play to *read*, as some Shakespeare plays are; it must be seen—not too early in life and not too often. If it is well acted and well produced, preferably in an open-air theatre on a fine summer evening, it gives up its magic. If it is studied in the school editions of scholars who either have no ear for magic or who mistakenly believe that its delicate and subtle pictures of romance in an English countryside can be "explained" and "taught", then it can become a deadly bore. What is much worse is that boys and girls who have to suffer its boredom conceive a dislike, or at best a suspicion, of "Shakespeare" in general.

TWELFTH NIGHT

This is an even more brilliant comedy than its predecessors and has always been one of the most popular of Shakespeare's plays. There is far more plot and action in it than in *As You Like It*; the humour is more vigorous and noisy; and the poetry is of that eternal loveliness that appeals to people of all ages and seems to strike afresh every time it is heard or read.

It opens in the vaguest of all places, "A city in Illyria", with Duke Orsino lamenting that the recently bereaved Olivia, who intends to mourn seven years for her brother, will not listen to any messages of love. The scene shifts to the sea-coast, where Viola, saved from shipwreck and thinking her brother drowned, determines to ask Duke Orsino to employ her as a page, for which she will dress in boy's clothes.

The Duke employs her and sends her to Olivia with his love messages—but the worst possible happens. Olivia, thinking Viola to be a boy, falls in love with "him"; while Viola herself, as a woman, falls in love with the Duke.

Olivia has an entertaining mixture of servants and guests in her house. There is Malvolio, "sick of self-love", who is her steward; there is her uncle, Sir Toby Belch, who loves a good drink and a rousing song; there is Sir Andrew Aguecheek, a fool of a man who hopes to secure the support of his friend Sir Toby in seeking the hand of Olivia; there is Maria, Olivia's maid, cheeky, good-humoured and intelligent; and there is the jester, Feste, who can sing a good song. Malvolio sternly rebukes Sir Toby and his companions for making too much noise and the "gang" decide to play a trick on him. With the aid of Maria they forge a letter for Malvolio to find, from which it appears that his mistress is in love with him and likes especially to see him dressed in a certain strange way. He duly appears before Olivia and behaves so strangely that she thinks he has gone mad and has him locked up.

Meanwhile the situation between the Duke, Viola and Olivia is becoming more and more tense. It is solved, however, in a very distressing way when Viola's brother, Sebastian, arrives on the scene,

*Malvolio*

having been saved also from the shipwreck. He and Viola are very much alike and of course everybody mistakes Sebastian for Viola. Sir Andrew, at Sir Toby's instigation, has challenged Viola to a duel and, seeing Sebastian, proceeds to "draw". Of course Sebastian beats him. The clown slips off to tell Olivia and Sir Toby is just beginning to fight Sebastian in Sir Andrew's defence when Olivia comes on the scene, despatches Sir Toby and his friends and marches off with Sebastian, thinking he is Viola. This time she will brook no argument and easily persuades Sebastian to marry her. Sir Toby is complaining to Viola about her treatment of Sir Andrew and Viola is protesting her innocence when Olivia and Sebastian appear. Brother and sister embrace with joy, Olivia realises what has happened and seems quite satisfied to accept Sebastian for a husband instead of Viola, and the Duke makes the best of a bad job by marrying Viola.

Sir Andrew is sent packing but Sir Toby, after being reprimanded for the trick played on Malvolio, marries Maria.

Malvolio is released from prison and goes away vowing to be revenged, but the play ends happily with a song from the jester.

Many believe *Twelfth Night* to be the world's greatest comedy, and it is certainly the best of Shakespeare's comedies. In the course of the next few years he was to write two or three bitter plays which are seldom performed today and which are classified as comedies only because they are obviously not tragedies. These few plays—*Troilus and Cressida, All's Well that Ends Well* and *Measure for Measure*—contain many noble scenes and splendid speeches, but they are not easy plays to follow and they leave unpleasant tastes and uncomfortable feelings after one has finished reading them. The fascinating thing about them, however, is that they were followed by the great string of tragedies which began with *Hamlet*. It was as though Shakespeare, having decided he had done all he could in the way of light-hearted comedy, had to work certain unpleasant things out of his system before he began to write the noblest of all his creations.

29

# IV. The Histories

GENERAL

## GENERAL

To a generation that thinks of history as a "subject" which has to be studied at school and taken at examinations, it seems strange that a popular dramatist should choose to write so many plays based on English history, and stranger still that a sufficient number of ordinary people should want to see such plays to make it worth the manager's effort to put them on. (We frequently have to remind ourselves that Shakespeare and his fellow-managers were in show business for profit, no less than playwrights and managers are today.)

But there are several explanations. The first, as already hinted, is that English history was *not* a school subject in the Elizabethan schools. People did not therefore approach an historical play with the thought that it might prove as boring as the things they had tried to study at school. Many of Shakespeare's audiences had never even been to school.

Another point to remember is that in the sixteenth and early seventeenth centuries the events portrayed in Shakespeare's historical plays were three hundred years more recent than they are today. Ballad-singers, minstrels and tellers of stories on long candle-lit evenings by the fireside had to rely far more than do our modern novelists and journalists on the happenings of old times, happenings that had been passed down from one generation to another, from mouth to mouth. The past, then, even what we should consider the comparatively remote past, was more real and vivid to Shakespeare's generation than it is to ours.

Most important of all, however, was the astounding growth of national feeling in England, which was partly a result of the exploits of Drake and the other explorers and adventurers, partly a result of the successful war against Spain, culminating in the defeat of the Spanish Armada in 1588. It was more noticeable in the towns, especially London, than in the country, and among the merchant classes and the educated people than among the poorer and labouring classes; but Shakespeare's audiences must have contained hundreds of people who were just beginning to realise that they were English, and that to be English was something to be proud of. From pride in one's country it is only a short step to interest in one's country's history.

## RICHARD III

The first historical play for which Shakespeare was solely responsible was, of all his Histories, the most "recent". The defeat of Richard III led to the accession of the Tudors, and Elizabeth I was only the fifth of that line. It was only to be expected that Shakespeare would paint the enemy of the Tudors in black colours. Recent historians have done much to prove that Richard III was not so black as he was painted, but there was little room for doubt in Shakespeare's portrait. The King, mentally warped by his physical deformity, announces that he is "determined to be a villain"; friends, rivals, advisers, even the famous "princes in the Tower" are cleared out of his way ruthlessly. But, as we saw with Shylock, Shakespeare was too great an artist to deprive his villain of all good traits; very few human beings are totally good, or totally evil, and there are moments when we admire Richard and even pity him.

This play (which returned to popularity in the nineteen-fifties after long neglect) is seen to be one of his earliest by the nature of the verse. Much of it is rhymed and much of it has the grand, rather pompous, style which was popular at the time and had been made popular by Christopher Marlowe—who also wrote historical plays.

### KING JOHN

It may seem strange that Shakespeare should go back to the 13th century for his next historical subject, but there were good reasons; in fact there had been at least two plays about King John in the sixteenth century before this one. We think of John as a "bad" king; to the Elizabethans he was something more. England was now strongly Protestant. Henry VIII's motives for leaving the Roman faith may have had little to do with religion, but his country had accepted his lead in the end; the short and lurid reign of Mary Tudor and the threat of invasion by the Catholic Spaniard had confirmed England in her Protestantism. Now there had once been another king who had stood out against the Pope— which meant, for Elizabethans, against Roman Catholicism. That king was John. His stand was not particularly glorious and his other acts were no credit either to his country or to his religion; but the Elizabethans were prepared to forgive much to anybody who opposed the Pope.

Shakespeare had little use for this kind of religious squabbling, however. The opposition to Rome, which probably figured large in the earlier "King John" plays, is played down in Shakespeare's, and in the scenes with the Papal Legate, Cardinal Pandulph, we find ourselves sympathising as much with him as with the King. To some extent the King has forfeited our support by ordering the murder of his rival to the throne, the young Prince Arthur; but there are glimpses of greatness in him which Shakespeare seems to have borrowed from one of the earlier plays on the subject.

*King John* is seldom acted nowadays and seldom, if ever, "done" in schools. Fortunately it is a good play to read; the terrible scene in which the King suggests to Hubert that he would like Arthur killed; the next scene, in which Arthur pleads to Hubert not to put out his eyes;

ARTHUR: *O, save me, Hubert, save me!*
(*King John*, IV, i, 73)

31

the noble grief of Queen Constance; the bluff Englishness of Faulconbridge and his famous lines at the end of the play—

> This England never did, nor never shall,
>
> Lie at the proud foot of a conqueror . . .

—these are only a few of the play's splendid moments. Incidentally, although its full title is *The Life and Death of King John*, it contains no mention of the signing of Magna Carta.

## RICHARD II

The trouble about dividing Shakespeare's plays into Comedies, Histories and Tragedies is that some of them belong to more than one category. *Richard II* is a case in point. It is a tragedy if ever there was one—a tragedy of weakness opposed to strength, of the man of words against the man of action. No doubt it was better for England that the wayward Richard, the boy-king who refused to grow up, the man of charm, should give way to the masterful Bolingbroke, the adult, the man who set himself an objective and did not allow himself to be distracted from reaching it. Yet it is impossible not to pity the King as we see him heading for disaster—a disaster which is largely of his own making. A first-rate actor in the part can make his audience feel that even if Richard *is* a failure as a king it is still a crime to kill him, even to depose him. Poetry may not win battles or build empires, we feel, but it is all the same a cause worth fighting for. The bluff, practical Bolingbroke will get things done, of course; he will tidy England up in his efficient way and no

doubt he will rule firmly and justly. But there are other values—spiritual values, if you like—which will be sacrificed in the process.

It is part of Shakespeare's skill that he gets us thinking like this and sympathising with the unheroic Richard, who was obviously not really deserving of our sympathy; and he does it mainly through poetry. The King uses lovely words and poetic ideas as a screen to hide behind, to protect himself against the impact of hard facts. One of the saddest moments in the Histories is when Richard realises that Bolingbroke is winning the support of the people. Richard does not seize his sword or wave a standard or make a rousing speech; he says

> For God's sake let us sit upon the ground,
>
> And tell sad stories of the death of kings.

If it were not so tragic it would be laughable; but it *is* tragic; we recognise it as one more step by the King towards his own deposition and death; and we do not laugh.

*Richard II* was considered a dangerous play towards the end of the century. Elizabeth was outliving her great popularity in some hearts. The country was "growing up" fast but the Queen continued to treat it as a child. Both in and out of Parliament men were getting restless and in 1601 Essex, having failed to carry out the Royal Command to subdue the Irish (easier said than done!) and fearing the results of his failure, plotted a rebellion against the Queen. On the night before the rebellion the Lord Chamberlain's Players gave *Richard II*, complete. That may not seem significant,

RICHARD: *I give this heavy weight from off my head,*
*And this unwieldy sceptre from my hand . . .*
*(Richard the Second, IV, i, 204)*

but it was. Ever since the play was first produced (1595 or 1596) the Queen had been convinced that the deposition scene at the end was a hit at her. "Wot ye not that I am Richard?" she wrote in a letter, and, whether at her command or not, the deposition scene was always omitted during her lifetime. Its inclusion on the eve of the rebellion—in fact the mere performance of that particular play—must have been a risky business for all concerned. Fortunately the Lord Chamberlain himself was a trusted friend of the Queen and perhaps he interceded for his Players. At any rate it does not appear that they were in any way punished, although Essex was put to death when his conspiracy was discovered.

### KING HENRY IV, PART I

In this play Bolingbroke, whom we saw ascend to power and kingship in *Richard II*, is having his own troubles. A strong opposition, led by Percy, Earl of Northumberland, and his son Hotspur, has rebelled against him. (The Percys had a sound claim to the throne.) Nearer home, his son—the future Henry V—is causing him some anxiety by his friendship with low-class frequenters of London pubs. The King himself has lost much of that dignity which marked him in *Richard II* and is in poor health.

But it is very easy to forget King Henry IV for large parts of this play and its successor. There is the young Prince Hal and there is Hotspur—one of Shakespeare's most brilliant creations. Above all, there is Falstaff.

### FALSTAFF

Once he reached his full power, Shakespeare never forgot that "the web of our life is of a mingled yarn, good and ill

33

together", as one of his own characters says. We have seen that there are moments of seriousness, almost of tragedy, in his best comedies; in the same way there is often humour mixed with the pathos in some of his great tragedies. Life is indeed for most people a mixture of joy and sorrow.

It is not surprising, therefore, to find some of the most amusing comedy in the historical plays. Not only was it advisable to "break up" the straightforward history with some light relief; it was even more necessary to present the historical period as a whole—and the whole included the ordinary men and women as well as the royalty, the nobility as well as the common soldiers. Sir John Falstaff, who first appeared in *King Henry IV, Part I*, represents (despite his knighthood) the lower ranks of society. Perhaps it would be truer to say that he represents nobody but himself, as he is certainly unique; but the company he keeps, and the places where he keeps it, are poles apart from the Court, the Palace and the Officers' Mess.

DOLL TEARSHEET: *Alas, poor ape, how thou sweat'st!* (*King Henry IV, Part II, II, iv,* 232)

He has been praised for his wit, and there are enough witty speeches of his to justify the praise. Yet it is not primarily as a wit that he lives in many people's hearts; it is rather as a lovable old rogue. He gets into trouble, and then out of it again, as easily as a bad boy, but both the getting in and the getting out are marked by glorious bluff and hilarious laughter. His fun is sometimes subtle, sometimes coarse; he is a splendid liar; he is a cheat and a coward; yet all these things are forgiven him because he makes us laugh and because he bears nobody any ill will.

### KING HENRY IV, PART II

The character of the young Prince Henry, in this play and its predecessor ("Part I") is not easy to assess. The Elizabethans saw him as a hero, the victor of Agincourt and the embodiment of all the manly British virtues. We find it difficult to admire him without some qualifications. In Part I we see him chastened by his father's rebuke and promising to live more as befits a great King's son; but in Part II he is back again with Falstaff and his tavern companions. It is true that he pulled himself together for a while in Part I and killed Hotspur in fair fight yet throughout that play one has the feeling that Hotspur is a better man than Harry. In Part I he plays a game with Falstaff in which he pretends he is King; and in Part II, while his father lies dying, he borrows the crown to try it on in another room. (He manages to persuade his father that he had a good and serious reason, but the incident leaves an unpleasant impression.) Worst of all is his rejection of Falstaff after he has been crowned. It was necessary, of

KING: *Once more unto the breach, dear friends, once more . . . (King Henry V, III, i, 1)*

course, to break away from the old associations and to make the cut clean; but his manner of doing it was heartless.

Sir John and his friends are standing in the crowd to welcome Henry V as he passes by. At first, when they shout a greeting to him, he merely asks the Lord Chief Justice to "speak to that vain man." Falstaff is astounded. "My king! my Jove!" he says, "I speak to thee, my heart." And the new King says:

> I know thee not, old man: fall to
>    thy prayers;
> How ill white hairs become a fool
>    and jester!

and so on, for twenty-five lines of priggish sermonising. Sir John, ashamed for his young Prince, puts a brave face on it. "I shall be sent for in private to him," he says (whether he believes it or not); "look you, he must seem thus to the world. . . . I shall be sent for soon at night." But the words are hardly spoken before the Lord Chief Justice returns with officers and Sir John is arrested. We are told that the King intends to see that his old friends are provided for but they are all to be banished until their behaviour has improved. When we remember how much the Prince had enjoyed their company in the past we find it difficult to forgive him—not, indeed, for what he did; that was no doubt necessary; but for the cruel way in which he did it.

### KING HENRY V

But the hero-king comes into his own in this play, which brings to an end the cycle of plays which began with *Richard II*. In an Epilogue to *Henry IV, Part II* Shakespeare had promised to bring back Falstaff, but he seems to have thought better of it;* we see no more of the fat rogue and even his death is reported, not presented to us. The experiences in The Boar's Head Tavern, however, were not altogether wasted; Henry, as King, made good use of the ability which he acquired

*There is evidence that Shakespeare intended to show Falstaff in France with the army but was prevented from doing so. He therefore killed him off early in *Henry V*.

35

as Prince to talk with the common people. Some of the best parts of *Henry V* are the scenes in which he talks easily, as one of themselves, to his soldiers just before the battle of Agincourt. He is their leader; he is their King; but he shows also that he is a man, as they are men. It is obvious, too, that they respect the man in him, just as they honour the King.

But when all's said and done, *Henry V* is a national epic, a sort of dramatic hymn of praise and thanksgiving for the resounding victory of Agincourt. It was for this that Richard II had to be deposed and murdered, that Henry IV had to quell the powerful Percy family, and his son to kill Hotspur in battle; it was for this, even, that Prince Hal had to play tough games with street louts and bandy dirty jokes with a greasy old soak named Falstaff. Everything was leading to the emergence of the national hero, all things to all men, and to the incredible victory against all the odds at Agincourt. *Henry V* is in many ways a less brilliant play than *Richard II* and the two parts of *Henry IV*; it lacks the poetry of the former and the crowded variety of the latter. Yet it is grander, more stirring, nobler, even, than the others. It had, after all, a nobler theme in the Battle of Agincourt, and Shakespeare was the man to match such a theme with stirring speech. It has always been a popular play with the English, especially in times of war; and although it has probably been studied in school more intensely even than *As You Like It*, it still draws the crowds to the theatre as it did in Shakespeare's own day.

# V. The Tragedies

### ROMEO AND JULIET

This was Shakespeare's first tragedy and in its earliest version was written before he was thirty. It is the pitiful story of the "star-crossed lovers" which has made it so popular, of course, but there are other characters who are not less striking, notably the vulgar and garrulous Nurse and the quick-witted and fiery young gallant, Mercutio.

The two great families of Verona, the Montagues and the Capulets, have quarrelled bitterly. Young Romeo Montague, mooning around love-sick for a dark girl named Rosaline, sees Juliet Capulet at a dance and falls in love with her at sight. He goes at night to her garden and learns that she loves him. Next day they are married secretly by Friar Laurence. In a fight in the street, Romeo's friend, Mercutio, is killed by Tybalt, a cousin of Juliet's, and Romeo kills Tybalt in revenge. As a result he has to run away from Verona.

Juliet's parents have arranged for her to marry Count Paris and are angry when she will not—although she cannot explain her refusal. In despair she consults Friar Laurence. His kind-hearted sympathy with the young lovers leads him to devise a foolish plot. He gives her a "potion" which will send her into so deep

JULIET: *Good night, good night! Parting
is such sweet sorrow.
That I shall say good night till it be morrow.*
(*Romeo and Juliet*, II, ii, 184–5)

a trance that she will appear to be dead.
After she has been buried in the family
vault he will secretly bring her a draught
which will revive her and she will then
be taken to where Romeo is hiding in
exile. Unfortunately the letter he writes
to Romeo explaining the stratagem never
reaches him.

Juliet's parents are distracted at her
"death"—the news of which reaches
Romeo. He buys some deadly poison for
himself and makes his way to Juliet's
family tomb. There he meets Count
Paris, who is genuinely distressed at
Juliet's death. They fight, and Paris is
killed. Romeo takes the poison he has
brought and dies on what he believes to
be the corpse of his beloved. The Friar,
coming to revive Juliet, sees the bodies
and runs away, although Juliet, who has
begun to revive, will not go with him.
She finds Romeo's body and, in despair,
kisses his poisoned lips and stabs herself
with his dagger. The parents of the two
young people meet at the tomb and, in
the grief which they share, are reconciled.

Shakespeare did not invent the story
but he vastly improved on what he
"borrowed". Above all he transfigured
the story by his gift for conveying high
romantic passion and by his command of
language. Romeo and his Juliet are the
most famous of all lovers on the stage
and they pour out their hearts' deep
longing—and later their almost un-
speakable sorrow—in words that haunt
the memory long after the play has been
seen or read. The balcony scene is well-
known; less well-known, perhaps, but not
less beautiful, are parts of Romeo's last
speech:

Death, that hath suck'd the honey of
thy breath,
Hath had no power yet upon thy
beauty:
Thou art not conquer'd; beauty's
ensign yet
Is crimson in thy lips and in thy
cheeks,
And death's pale flag is not advanced
there. . . .

It *is* beautiful . . . and yet there
seems to be something wrong. Would
Romeo—would any young man—talk like
this at such a moment? Is it sincere? Does
it not seem artificial, stagey? We can
believe in the Nurse; we can believe in
Mercutio; they really do speak and act
like the kind of human beings we know;
but can we really believe in Romeo (or in
Juliet either, for that matter)?

The answer is in the first sentence of

37

this chapter—it was Shakespeare's first tragedy and parts of it were written while he was in his twenties. It is highly romantic of course; it is theatrical and improbable and artificial; but it is 'prentice work. Shakespeare will do better than this; but he will not often reach such heights of sustained, emotional, magical poetry.

## JULIUS CAESAR

The Elizabethans were profoundly interested in Roman history and this interest was maintained until well into the 18th century. After that the interest waned and today only scholars are familiar with the names and events which were almost household words in Shakespeare's day.

Perhaps the first Elizabethans realised that the England of their day had much in common with Rome at its greatest. Their Queen ruled with the wisdom and autocracy of the best Roman Emperors; their country was prosperous and was beginning to be respected, and even feared, abroad as was Rome; they loved high-sounding oratory as the Romans did; the more educated and sophisticated were beginning to acquire a truly Roman love for good food, good wine, physical strength—and cruel sports. At school they had read the Roman poets and historians and orators . . . Whatever the reasons may have been, there is no doubt that books like Plutarch's *Lives* was widely read and plays on Roman themes extremely popular. Shakespeare's *Julius Caesar* was probably written about 1600, but there had been other plays on the subject before.

The plot is simple. Caesar's victory over his Roman rival, Pompey, has turned his head. There are rumours that he is thinking of persuading the Senate to crown him King, and the Romans have bitter memories of earlier experiments in the rule of Kings. Cassius, who is jealous of Caesar's popularity, cleverly plans a conspiracy. He mentions to the "noble Brutus" the prevalent rumour about the approaching crowning of Caesar and reminds him how his ancestors put down Tarquin, an ancient King of Rome, to save the City from bloodshed and civil strife. Cassius enlists more conspirators (using Brutus's name as a bait) and the plotters meet in Brutus's garden at night. They decide to murder Caesar as he goes to a meeting of the Senate at the Capitol. Cassius wants Antony killed too, but Brutus will not hear of it; it is necessary for Rome's sake, he argues, that Caesar shall be sacrificed but they would be mere butchers if they went further than that.

The plot nearly misfires as Caesar's wife, Calpurnia, has bad dreams which, she believes, signify Caesar's murder and she almost persuades him not to go out at all that day. But one of the conspirators cleverly overrules her arguments by playing upon Caesar's vanity. He goes—and is assassinated.

Brutus makes a short speech to the crowd explaining why he has killed his friend, and the crowd is impressed and hails Brutus as Rome's saviour. Then Antony addresses the crowd; he has asked Brutus's permission to pay a last tribute to his friend and, despite Cassius's objections, Brutus has given him leave. The result—for Brutus—is fatal. By the time Antony has finished his brilliantly convincing oration the crowd is thirsting for the conspirators' blood.

CAESAR: *Et tu, Brute? Then fall, Caesar!*
(*Julius Caesar, III, i, 77*).

Antony, Lepidus and Octavius Caesar take over the running of the City and lead out the army to put down the rebellion of Brutus, Cassius and their friends. In the camp at Philippi Brutus and Cassius have a bitter quarrel over a trifle, but make it up. They plan the attack on Antony's army and when Cassius sees that Brutus is making a mistake he points it out; but he does not press the point— possibly because they have so recently patched up their quarrel. But Brutus's plan of campaign duly fails. A tragic error leads to the suicide of Cassius; Brutus is captured; he has a chance to escape but refuses it and he, too, in the Roman fashion, runs on his own sword and dies.

Many people feel that *Julius Caesar* suffers because the assassination and the speeches in the Capitol, which occur in Act III, make so great a climax that the last two Acts must necessarily seem tame —something of an anti-climax. There is something in this criticism, but not so much as you might think. After all, Shakespeare called the play *Julius Caesar*, not "Brutus and Antony" or "The Tragedy of Brutus." Caesar was meant to be the heart and centre of the tragedy even although he was killed in Act III. What Shakespeare intended, no doubt, is that we should realise that Caesar dead was as vital to the plot as Caesar living; and the spirit of Caesar broods over Acts IV and V. He is never entirely absent from the thoughts of Brutus and Cassius in their quarrel; Octavius reminds Brutus and Cassius, at their parley before the battle, of the reason why they are at war; Cassius's last words are:

> Caesar, thou art revenged,
> Even with the sword that kill'd thee.

When Brutus learns of the disaster he says

> O Julius Caesar, thou art mighty yet!
> Thy spirit walks abroad . . .

and as he dies he seeks to lay the ghost he has raised:

> Caesar, now be still:
> I killed not thee with half so good a will.

If we had not been so excited during that mighty Capitol scene in Act III we should have realised that Julius Caesar remained the most important figure in the play, though not the hero; but the scene ran away with Shakespeare and the result is that the whole balance seems to be shifted. Shakespeare still had something to learn, but he never again made the mistake of over-weighting a play in

39

the middle. (We can be glad that he did it, all the same, for he never again wrote such a magnificently sustained piece of mob-oratory as Antony's speech.)

The other outstanding characters are Brutus and Cassius—and the Roman mob. Brutus is called "noble" by the others and Antony pays him a dignified and magnanimous tribute at the end. To modern audiences he appears, perhaps, a little *too* noble—a trifle priggish now and then—and certainly obstinate in his virtuousness. Three times he failed to take the practical advice of the less scrupulous Cassius, and each time he suffered for it; once, when he would not agree to the assassination of Antony, the second time when he allowed Antony to address the mob, and finally when drawing up the plan of campaign at Philippi. But we see a more lovable side of his nature in his conversations with his wife and with his servant, Lucius. Cassius, on the other hand, is made of more normal human stuff. He is envious, cunning, worldly-wise and as sharp as a needle. But he had his redeeming features; he was apparently devoted to Brutus, and he was a soldier with long and loyal service to Rome.

But the play abounds with sharply-drawn life-like characters, many of them built up by Shakespeare from a bare reference in a sentence or even a few words in North's translation of Plutarch's *Lives* from which he drew his facts. And all through the play we are being reminded of the fickleness of the common people who made up the mob. It is a mistake to attribute to Shakespeare the opinions expressed by this or that character in his plays, but it is safe to assume that he hated and despised "the mob".

Not only is *Hamlet* Shakespeare's greatest play: it is one of the great plays of all time. It is the first of the series of monumental tragedies in which Shakespeare looks into the darkest corners of the human mind and explores the saddest depths of human misery.

The plot—taken from a variety of old legends and early plays—is misleadingly simple. Hamlet is the son of Queen Gertrude and King Hamlet but his father has recently died and his mother has married again. Her new husband is Hamlet's uncle, Claudius, brother to the dead king. The ghost of his father appears on the battlements of the royal castle at Elsinore and reveals that he was murdered by Claudius, with the connivance of Gertrude. He makes Hamlet swear to revenge his murder. The knowledge of the crime has a deep effect on Hamlet; he behaves so strangely that Gertrude and Claudius first suspect that he is mad and then

HAMLET: *Thou wretched, rash, intruding fool, farewell!*
*I took thee for thy better.*
(*Hamlet, III, iv*, 31–2)

suspect that he knows their secret. He leaves them in no doubt about the latter point by persuading some strolling actors to perform a play in which the murder of his father is re-enacted.

Hamlet has loved Ophelia, daughter of a courtier, Polonius, and sister of Laertes. Ophelia is distraught by Hamlet's insane treatment of her and eventually drowns herself; while Polonius, spying behind a curtain while Hamlet is talking with his mother, is run through by Hamlet's sword.

Claudius sees an opportunity, in this latest crime, to get rid of Hamlet. He says that he is in danger with the people because of his killing of Polonius and sends him to England with two courtiers who have secret instructions to kill him. Hamlet discovers the plot and returns to Denmark where Laertes, thirsting to avenge the death of his father and his sister, is waiting for him. Claudius persuades him to challenge Hamlet to a fencing match, but he puts poison on Laertes' foil and prepares a cup of poison for Hamlet to drink in case his first trick fails. Hamlet is wounded but in the scuffle he and Laertes exchange foils. Laertes dies of his wound and Gertrude unknowingly drinks the poisoned wine. Hamlet also is mortally wounded but before he dies he realises his uncle's treachery and stabs him.

The story, told like that, seems cheap and melodramatic. The genius of Shakespeare made a great and noble tragedy out of this second-rate material by presenting it as the mental struggle of a sensitive and highly intelligent young man who is torn between terrible alternatives. As a dutiful and loving son he is bitterly and profoundly shocked by his father's murder and his mother's too hasty re-marriage. To do nothing about it, especially after the intervention of his father's ghost, seems unthinkable. On the other hand his finer nature tells him that it is wrong to meet murder with murder, treachery with treachery. As the time goes by and the crime remains unavenged he despises himself more and more. He sees one of the troop of players work himself into a fine frenzy over a purely fictitious character; yet he, Hamlet, with such a real cause for frenzy, cannot bring himself to act. Once he catches his uncle on his knees, trying to pray for forgiveness; he comes upon him from behind; it is a perfect opportunity to kill him on the instant; but he cannot do it.

Yet although Hamlet himself declares he is "pigeon-liver'd", that he thinks and talks too much instead of getting on with the job, it would be wrong to think of him as weak or "soft". The use of the actors to stage a play which would "prove" his uncle's guilt was a definite, practical step. The killing of Polonius may have been rash but it was the instantaneous reflex of a man of action. On board the ship he stole the letters of his companions while they slept—letters which would have led to his death—and substituted others, which he had forged; when the ship was attacked by pirates he was the only one who boarded the attacking ship. In the final scene he showed himself a skilful fencer and a quick thinker. None of this is the behaviour of a coward or a milksop. In fact it was precisely because he was normally a man of action—but a man of action who at the same time had a keen brain and a lively conscience—that he suffered his own private hell of indecision.*

Whatever Shakespeare intended us to think about Hamlet, there is no doubt that he wrote one of the finest character-studies in the world's literature—and also one of the finest parts an actor could ask for. But the play is not all Hamlet. The weak Gertrude; the villainous Claudius, who yet has moments of dawning remorse; the typical staunch friend, Horatio; the headstrong and fiery Laertes, who was certainly never in doubt as to what he should do; his father, Polonius, the wise but long-winded old courtier; the different hangers-on at court; the soldiers; the actors—all these and others help to fill a long list of characters who speak and act as they would in real life. The play is packed with action, but also with poetry and with searching observations on life, on good and evil, and on the ideas and motives which control our thoughts and actions.

To see *Hamlet* is not merely an entertainment; it is an experience—almost a duty. And it never palls. Every time one sees it, every time one reads it, one discovers something new, something one had never fully appreciated before. It is the highest point reached by the world's greatest dramatist.

### OTHELLO

This is not an easy play, especially for young people. It is often regarded as a tragedy of jealousy—which it is not—

but its heart and mainspring is the despair of a noble man and a great lover who believes that the woman he had thought perfect has deceived him, and his anger when he is convinced that his honour and self-respect have been lowered.

The scene is set mainly in Cyprus. Othello, a Moor and a successful general, is in love with Desdemona, daughter of a Venetian senator. He wins her hand by persuading her father of his integrity and of their great love for each other.

Iago, who is Othello's ensign, or standard-bearer—the lowest rank of officer—is jealous of Cassio, Othello's lieutenant. The marriage of his master suggests a way in which he can oust Cassio from his superior post. First he gets Cassio involved in a drunken quarrel which leads to Cassio's dismissal; then, when Cassio pleads with Desdemona to intercede for him, Iago quietly suggests to Othello that there is something between Cassio and Desdemona. Having sown the seed of suspicion he proceeds to take every opportunity that craft and luck put in his way until finally Othello, convinced of Desdemona's guilt, smothers her. When he learns the truth from Emilia, Iago's wife, he kills himself, but not before he has denounced Iago before representatives of the Senate who have visited Cyprus. Iago kills Emilia but is himself led away in chains, refusing to say a word.

The murder of Desdemona is a heart-rending scene but perhaps the greatest moment of the play comes immediately afterwards, when Emilia first realises the wickedness of Iago and tells the stricken Othello how he has been tricked.

*Othello* is not so much Shakespearean —except in its poetry—as Elizabethan.

OTHELLO: *Yet I'll not shed her blood,*
*Nor scar that whiter skin of hers than snow*
*And smooth as monumental alabaster.*

(*Othello, V, ii,* 3–5)

The sixteenth and seventeenth centuries were more accustomed than we are to the idea of utter villainy, as represented by Iago. We find it hard to believe that a man of Othello's intelligence could be so deceived and should know so little of his own officers as to suspect Cassio of intriguing with Desdemona and to believe everything Iago told him. It is tempting to believe that Shakespeare, with his deep knowledge of human nature, found it as hard to believe as we do. But he saw in the old Italian story the makings of a powerful tragedy, and he knew that most men and women of his day would be ready to swallow any improbabilities in the story provided his handling of it were sufficiently dramatic and his language sufficiently compelling.

### KING LEAR

Shakespeare found the story for this play in Holinshed's *Chronicles*, and perhaps in an earlier play by an unknown hand. As usual, the story is ennobled by his magic touch: *King Lear* is the most moving of his tragedies. Parts of it, when adequately played, can hardly be seen without tears.

King Lear is an old man. He has decided to divide his kingdom between his three daughters. It is his rather senile wish that the daughter who loves him most shall have the largest share. Goneril and Regan, the two older sisters, profess their love in extravagant terms; Cordelia, the youngest and most sincere (who really loves her father dearly), can only say, in some embarrassment, that she loves him as a daughter should. Lear curses her in his anger; she is banished from the Court and the King of France marries her without a dowry. Her portion is divided between Goneril and Regan on condition that each shall in turn keep the King and one hundred knights. The Earl of Kent takes Cordelia's part and is banished.

The Earl of Gloucester has two sons, Edmund, who is illegitimate, and Edgar. Edmund lies to his father about Edgar, who is therefore turned adrift. He disguises himself as a mad beggar.

Goneril and Regan show their true feelings by not keeping to the bargain about maintaining Lear and a hundred knights and finally by turning him out of doors in a storm. Gloucester tries to comfort the old King, who has lost his reason, and is betrayed by Edmund. Cornwall, husband of Regan, puts out Gloucester's eyes but is killed by a servant in the scuffle. Regan wants Edmund but Goneril has also made advances to him, so the sisters are now enemies. Edgar, unrecognised by his blinded father, takes care of him.

The King of France lands in England with Cordelia, intending to win back Lear's kingdom. Cordelia meets Lear and comforts him, but the British armies, under Edmund and Albany (Goneril's husband) defeat the French and both Lear and Cordelia are captured. Edmund's villainy is unmasked; Edgar comes forward to answer his challenge and mortally wounds him. News is brought that Goneril has poisoned Regan and killed herself. Before he dies Edmund confesses that he has given instructions for Lear and Cordelia to be killed; but his confession comes too late. Lear enters, carrying the body of Cordelia. He is still mad, but recognises his daughter and knows she is dead; then he too dies.

There is something of the fairy-tale about the story; if it began "Once upon a time there was an old king . . ." it would not seem strange. It is full of

LEAR: *Blow, winds, and crack your cheeks!*
(*King Lear, III, ii, 1*)

tenderness and deep human sympathy. The Fool, who faithfully remains with Lear in his adversity, is a pathetic shadow of the court jester. Edgar leading his blind old father has a sad sort of humour; Kent is a type frequent in Shakespeare—the vigorous, hearty man of action who shows under his bluffness an infinite capacity for loyalty and love. (One feels that Shakespeare must have had some good friends.) Cordelia wins our sympathy not only because of her harsh treatment by her father but because of her quiet undemonstrative love for him. In fact there is almost as much goodness and kindness in this tragedy as there is wickedness and crime.

Act IV, Scene vii, contains some of the loveliest passages. Lear awakes in captivity and finds his reason partly restored. He looks around him in wonder.

Pray, do not mock me:
I am a very foolish fond old man,

Fourscore and upward, not an hour
   more or less;
And, to deal plainly,
I fear I am not in my perfect mind.
   . . .

                  Do not laugh at me;
For, as I am a man, I think this lady
To be my child Cordelia.

And Cordelia answers, through her tears, "And so I am, I am." Later, when they are sent to prison by Edmund, Lear comforts his daughter with dreams of their future happiness:

We two alone will sing like birds i'
   the cage. . . .

There are fifty lines or so near the end of the last scene which are so heart-breaking that they have been called "too painful for tragedy." They must be seen, or read, as a whole and in their context.

## MACBETH

This has always been one of the most popular of the great tragedies, on the stage if not in the examination room. Shakespeare found the bare bones of the story in Holinshed and one can imagine him turning the pages feverishly in search of a suitable subject to fit the times. For the play was probably written in 1605 or 1606, and in 1603 the accession of James I (Scotland's James VI) not only united the two kingdoms but brought whole crowds of Scotsmen to London for the first time. With their "foreign" speech and their outlandish clothes they must have been a source of much amusement to Londoners and no doubt the subject of jokes and conversations and popular songs for a year or two. Shakespeare himself, or the proprietors of the theatre for which he was writing, could feel fairly

confident that a play based on Scottish history would provide a good "draw"— and Shakespeare knew where to look for inspiration.

But there are no signs of hack-work about *Macbeth*. Even its comparative brevity as it has come down to us may be due to a faulty version of the text. It is a powerful tragedy played out against a background of the supernatural. We are used to ghosts in Elizabethan drama, and in many plays of the period the unseen, unexplained world, behind or above or beneath the familiar world we know, is never far away. But *Macbeth* is full of the breath of this other world, even as Macbeth himself had "supp'd full with horrors."

The play opens in thunder and lightning in "a desert place", with sinister witches muttering darkly. They prophesy to Macbeth that he will be "thane of Cawdor" and "king hereafter". Banquo, who is with Macbeth, says to the witches,

THIRD WITCH: *All hail, Macbeth, that shalt be king hereafter!* (Macbeth, I, iii, 50)

45

in effect, "What about me?" and the witches answer: "Thou shalt get kings, though thou be none." Hardly have the witches disappeared when a messenger arrives from King Duncan to say that Macbeth is made Thane of Cawdor. He is amazed and excited; one prophecy is proved correct already, and if one, why not both? He writes to his wife telling her of the witches' words. She has hardly had time to read the letter and to make up her mind to egg on Macbeth to murder the King, when news comes that the King is coming to stay at Macbeth's castle that night. He arrives, attended by Macbeth, and that night he is murdered. His sons fly to England and Macbeth becomes King of Scotland. The witches' prophecies are fulfilled.

But he cannot forget that Banquo also heard the witches and that they proclaimed that he would "get kings" although he himself would never reign. To ensure his safety he plans the murder of Banquo and his son, but the son escapes. Banquo's ghost appears at Macbeth's table and the assembled lords, who may already have suspected Macbeth of Duncan's murder, must have felt their suspicions confirmed by Macbeth's distraught behaviour. Lady Macbeth attempts to rally her husband, and he visits the witches again. They warn him to beware Macduff, a loyal Scottish nobleman.

Macduff is aware of his dangerous position and escapes to England, but his wife and children are murdered on Macbeth's orders. Meanwhile Lady Macbeth breaks beneath the strain, goes mad, and dies. Macduff returns with Malcolm and an army to attempt to recover the throne.

LADY MACBETH: *Out, damned spot! out, I say!* (*Macbeth V, i,* 33)

At first Macbeth is confident of success; the witches have promised him immunity until two apparently impossible conditions are fulfilled. But the apparently impossible happens—and Macbeth, fighting bravely and desperately at the end, is killed.

We know Macbeth is wicked but we pity him. We feel he is not by nature ruthless but is misled by the evil witches and by a wife who shares his ambition but exceeds him in unscrupulousness. Each step leads him deeper into crime, until he admits that he has gone too far to return. He is weak and turns to the witches for further encouragement—which they seem to offer. So he must go on. In the end the gallant soldier, who had won "golden opinions" and in whom his king had had absolute trust, ends alone, defeated, and hated by everybody, including probably himself.

The poetry of the play is intense and haunting. Like Richard II, Macbeth turns his greatest anxieties into pure poetry, but where Richard uses lovely words as a sort of smoke-screen to cover his retreat from reality, Macbeth seems to draw inspiration or comfort from them. On the stage it sometimes seems that the poetry is lost in the speed and tenseness of the action; whether Shakespeare's audiences grasped all of its beauty and power it is impossible now to say, but for us, in our own day, *Macbeth* is a play to read as well as to see.

### ANTONY AND CLEOPATRA

In *Romeo and Juliet* we saw a tragedy of young love; this play deals with the havoc that passion can cause in the lives of mature people; and whereas the earlier was a private tragedy, almost a domestic affair, this is played out in public. The Antony who ruled the crowd so skilfully in *Julius Caesar* here finds it impossible to rule his own obsession with the magical Queen of Egypt. We know him to be a great and respected leader; yet in one act of treachery he betrays himself, his wife, and Rome.

The story, taken from Plutarch, can be told very briefly. It opens in Alexandria. Antony is already bewitched but the news from Rome calls him away. He promises Cleopatra he will return and cheers her with the news that his wife, Fulvia, is dead. While he is in Rome he makes a pact with Octavius Caesar which is sealed by his marriage to Octavius's sister, Octavia. When Cleopatra hears of this marriage she is furious, while Antony himself finds that he cannot stay away from his temptress. His return leads to war, in which the Roman fleet attacks Egypt. At the height of the battle Cleopatra breaks off the fight and turns her

ships for home, whereupon Antony turns and follows her. He is pursued to Alexandria by Caesar and a pitched battle takes place, in which Antony is at first successful. When he is subsequently defeated he believes he has again been betrayed by Cleopatra and banishes her from his sight. She sends word by a messenger that she is dead and Antony, defeated, shamed and deserted, falls upon his sword. He is carried, dying, to the "monument" where Cleopatra awaits him and is hauled up to her—in Shakespeare's theatre, to the balcony over the stage (see pp. 6–7). He dies in her arms and she, fearing lest she should be borne in triumph in Octavius Caesar's victory march, kills herself by embracing a venomous snake.

It is worth noting that when Dryden wrote a tragedy on the same theme about seventy years later he called it *All for Love, or the World Well Lost*.

This play brings to the fore a problem which is never far from the minds of those who read and study Shakespeare. As we have seen, the women's parts in his plays were acted by boys. He did his best for these boys; as often as possible he wrote parts for them which required a "girl" to masquerade as a "boy" and, as Mr Ivor Brown has pointed out, he never asked them to embrace or to kiss on the stage, except perhaps in formal greeting. Yet in Cleopatra he wrote a part which is charged with passion, a part, moreover, which even the most experienced actresses of our time find difficult to play just because it is so full of intense, *adult* emotion. One can only conclude that he knew what he was doing and that there must have been an outstanding

47

CLEOPATRA: *Come thou mortal wretch,*
*With thy sharp teeth this knot intrinsicate*
*Of life at once untie.* (*Antony and*
*Cleopatra*, V, ii, 306–8)

genius of a boy actor in his company for
whom he was writing.

The two main characters dominate
this play in a way which is unusual for
Shakespeare, but among the minor
characters, Enobarbus stands out. He is
a friend and follower of Antony, obviously
thinks highly of him and is devoted to his
service; but he criticises him and stands
up to him and eventually leaves him in
despair and goes over to Caesar. When
Antony hears of this he sends all Enobarbus's goods and possessions after him,
saying

> Write to him . . . gentle adieus and
> greetings;
> Say that I wish he never find more
> cause
> To change a master. O, my fortunes
> have
> Corrupted honest men! Dispatch.
> Enobarbus!

Such gentleness overwhelms Enobarbus.
He is seized with shame and kills himself

in a ditch . . . . It is a small incident,
but it tells us much about Antony.

The greatest glories of a glorious play
are in the love-passages or in shorter
outbursts of feeling inspired by love.
When Antony hears the false report of
Cleopatra's death he says to his man,
Eros,

> Unarm, Eros; the long day's task is
> done,
> And we must sleep;

and when Antony dies in Cleopatra's
arms she cries

> The crown o' the earth doth melt.
> My Lord!
> O, wither'd is the garland of the war,
> The soldier's pole is fall'n: young
> boys and girls
> Are level now with men; the odds
> is gone,
> And there is nothing left remarkable
> Beneath the visiting moon.

As with some of Macbeth's great speeches
we feel that what the words mean is of
secondary importance; enough that the
very sound of them can bind us like a
spell.

### CORIOLANUS

The last of the great tragedies was
based even more firmly than *Antony and
Cleopatra* on Plutarch. It tells of Marcius,
called "Coriolanus" because of his victory over the Volscians when he "flut-
tered their dovecotes at Corioli." Even
for a Roman he is proud—and politically
simple-minded. Flushed with victory he
stands for the consulship and is elected
on the strength of his military prowess,
although he can hardly be persuaded to
make the customary speeches to the
crowd. ("Bid them wash their faces and

keep their teeth clean," he says.) After his election, the two Tribunes—who resent his attitude—stir up the people, and he is driven from Rome. He goes to his enemy, Aufidius, the Volscian leader, to offer his services against his own city, and is accepted. He approaches the gates of the City as a conqueror and Rome is at his mercy. Senators and friends come to beg for mercy, but in vain. Then he sees at the entrance to his tent his wife, his small son and his mother; they are all in black. In a wonderful speech his mother alternately upbraids and implores him; he is defeated as much by her scorn as by her passionate entreaty and finally yields. He persuades Aufidius to make peace and so save Rome, but when he returns to Volscian territory he is declared a traitor and killed.

While we must feel some pity for Coriolanus in his death as a traitor, he wins our sympathy to a smaller degree than do Shakespeare's other great tragic heroes. To that extent *Coriolanus* is a lesser play, and it has never been a popular one. (Even in his own day it seems to have been a failure.) But it contains its glorious moments none the less. Coriolanus's speech to the crowd on his banishment reveals his contempt in words which seem to quiver with pride and anger:

> You common cry of curs! whose breath I hate
> As reek o' the rotten fens, whose loves I prize
> As the dead carcases of unburied men
> That do corrupt my air, *I* banish *you*. . . .
> . . . Despising,

For you, the city, thus I turn my back:
There is a world elsewhere.

But his speeches to his mother and his wife are in a nobler and gentler mood. The other characters, even down to the ordinary soldiers, are vividly and movingly drawn.

### CONCLUSION

These eight tragedies would by themselves establish Shakespeare as the greatest dramatist of all time. The first was a young man's experiment in writing, for him, something different; he will try anything once. The second, *Julius Caesar*, was sandwiched between his greatest comedies and his greatest histories. But the last six were all written between 1602 and 1609, when he was round about forty and passing through a period of profound mental disturbance. That is admittedly a conjecture, because we know of nothing which could have caused such a long period of depression or strain; but it is a reasonably safe conjecture. No man who was capable of writing *Twelfth Night* and *As You Like It* could suddenly switch from happy, light-hearted comedy to profound tragedy—and remain thus for eight years without writing a single *happy* play by way of relief—unless he was himself passing through a period of emotional or spiritual depression at the time. We know that he had no financial worries; we can be fairly sure that he was not just meeting a continued public demand for tragedies, since the last two or three were not well received and did not appear in print until years later. But what the explanation was we do not know and probably never shall.

49

# VI. Last Plays

## CYMBELINE

A clumsy, ill-constructed ending to a play written in comparative youth may be explained as the results of inexperience; when we come across such an ending in a play written—or at any rate produced—just after the run of great tragedies which Shakespeare wrote between 1600 and 1612, we must look for some other explanation. *Cymbeline* is such a play, and it can be explained. In the First Folio it is entered as a Tragedy, and the first part of it certainly promises a tragic ending. Then in the last act everybody seems to be reconciled to everybody else and the play finishes happily after all. Theories and convenient explanations are dangerous, yet it looks as though Shakespeare began *Cymbeline* during his "tragic period" but put it aside unfinished for some reason or other. Then came an urgent request from the management for another play—preferably *not* a tragedy. Shakespeare may well have been in retirement at Stratford when the request reached him, but wherever he was he picked up the discarded manuscript, altered it here and there perhaps, wrote a new last act and sent it along to the theatre.

Like so many of the stories of Shakespeare's plays, the story of Imogen, driven from home by a cruel stepmother and befriended by strangers in a cave, has a fairy-tale element, and the happy ending, although clumsily reached, suits it better than a tragic ending would. It also has some fine scenes and one lovely song.

## THE WINTER'S TALE

If *Cymbeline* is fairy-tale, this play is a novel, as full of plot as any modern thriller. The story is too complicated to be reduced to a few words, although it is never difficult to follow. For its glorious indifference to the matter-of-fact details of history and geography it is the most daring of all Shakespeare's plays. Parts of it are set in "Bohemia: a desert country near the sea," which leaves us guessing where Bohemia was supposed to be, since no country called Bohemia is either desert or "near the sea". There is a magnificent stage-direction, "Exit, pursued by a bear." In this sea-side Bohemia of no date, "twelve satyrs" dance, a "statue" comes to life, a travelling ballad-seller sells songs with names which a Shakespearean audience would recognise at once, a king consults the Delphic Oracle, and a lovely girl recites a list of typical English flowers—

> Daffodils,
> That come before the swallow dares,
>    and take
> The winds of March with beauty;
>    violets dim . . .
>                    pale primroses,
> That die unmarried. . . .
>                    bold oxlips and
> The crown imperial; lilies of all
>    kinds . . .

Yet although it is such a hotch-potch in its details it is a good play, full of the tenderness of a tale told by the fire on a winter's night, with a happy ending, a very English crowd of shepherds, and a

50

POLIXENES: *Pray, good shepherd, what fair swain is this*
*Which dances with your daughter? (Winter's Tale, IV, iv, 166)*

lovable heroine who does not appear until Act III.

## THE TEMPEST

This was probably the last play which Shakespeare wrote and it bears all the marks of a great man's maturity. He returns to the world of magic which he first explored as a young man in *A Midsummer Night's Dream*, but he returns to it with nearly twenty years of crowded life behind him. Instead of the carefree Puck we have the troubled Ariel, working faithfully enough for his master, Prospero, but working for his freedom. The other supernatural (or at least sub-human) inhabitant of Prospero's island is no fairy but a sinister monster, Caliban.

Prospero lives on this island with his daughter, Miranda. Years ago, when Miranda was a child, he had been driven from his dukedom of Milan by Antonio, his brother. Already interested in magic, he had taken his books with him and spent his time on the island perfecting his art. Now he is able to take his revenge. His brother, accompanied by the King of Naples and the latter's son, Ferdinand, is on the way to a wedding in Tunis, and Prospero, with the help of Ariel, arranges that the party shall be wrecked on his island. Miranda and Ferdinand fall in love, while Prospero, confronted with his usurping brother, is content merely to bury the past and be reconciled.

There is something here for all tastes— magic, romance, the broad humour of the shipwrecked servants in various comic situations, songs, dances and pageantry. The play opens with a shipwreck (and goodness knows how *that* was portrayed on the stage in 1611 or so) and includes

MIRANDA:                  *O dear father,*
*Make not too rash a trial of him, for*
*He's gentle, and not fearful.*
                  (*The Tempest,* I, ii, 466–68).

a transformation scene and a masque;* no wonder it was popular!

For some reason best known to producers, Prospero is usually presented as an old man with a long white beard. Miranda is only fifteen or sixteen and her father could have been a mere thirty-five to forty. But the impression of age lends weight, perhaps, to what is usually regarded as Shakespeare's own farewell to the stage. Prospero has instructed Ariel

---

*A Masque was a short, rather formal little play within a play, very popular in James I's day. Gods and goddesses usually appeared and sang, or recited to music. Dresses were costly and, wherever possible, there was an elaborate setting. As time went on the Masque was separated from the "parent" play and became a self-contained art on its own.

to release his "prisoners" (the shipwrecked party) and after the Spirit has gone he muses on his use of the art of magic. Then he says:

> But this rough magic
> I here abjure. . . .
>                  . . . I'll break my staff,
> Bury it certain fathoms in the earth,
> And deeper than did ever plummet
>     sound
> I'll drown my book.

### KING HENRY VIII

Did Shakespeare adhere to his intention to "drown his book"? We shall never know for certain, but a year or two after *The Tempest* a new play, *King Henry VIII*, was presented at the Globe Theatre and this play was included in the First Folio as one of Shakespeare's. (The performance was notable; in Act I a round of gunfire announced the arrival of the King, in disguise, at a party given by Wolsey. The shot set fire to the thatch and the theatre was burnt down.) Most critics agree that this play was only partly the work of Shakespeare, and for all we know his part may have been written years before.

The great speeches of Wolsey's in Act III were almost certainly written by Fletcher. They have the noble sweep and glory of Shakespeare at his best; and they are almost the only lines in *Henry VIII* which are well known. The great man was certainly wise to retire when new playwrights were appearing who could write so well as this.

# VII. Other Plays

Every now and then an ambitious theatre manager decides to present the whole Shakespeare output; Mr Nugent Monck did it at his Maddermarket Theatre in Norwich, the Old Vic Company have done it in London, and various University and Repertory Companies have done it in the U.S.A. But it is an act of homage rather than a compliment to Shakespeare—or to the theatre's patrons. Some of the plays attributed to Shakespeare are not good entertainment today.

There is *Titus Andronicus*, for example, a gory tragedy which was immensely popular in the sixteenth and seventeenth centuries but which our queasy stomachs find too nauseating today. There are the so-called "bitter comedies", like *All's Well that Ends Well*, *Measure for Measure* and *Troilus and Cressida*. Scholars who read these plays—because they have few chances to see them acted—find their reward; they have their great moments of true Shakespearean insight into human nature, scenes and speeches which only Shakespeare could have written. But, without being tragic, they lack that clear gaiety which marks Shakespearean comedy and they leave a bitter taste. Also there are the plays for which Shakespeare was only partly responsible—*Pericles*, the three Parts of *King Henry VI*, *Timon of Athens*. These again have their great moments; if we had never had *Hamlet* or *Richard II* or *Twelfth Night* we should no doubt have hailed these minor, part-Shakespearean works as masterpieces; as

it is, we write them down as pot-boilers or hack-work—although that is hardly the word we should use of, say, *Pericles* had any other dramatist written it.

But they are vitally important if we are to understand the man Shakespeare himself. It is often suggested that genius is concerned only with great ideas, that it moves serenely above the heads of ordinary mortals and cannot be bothered with practical everyday problems. Nothing is further from the true genius than this ridiculous notion, and Shakespeare was the genius who did most to disprove it. Apart from his work as part-owner and part-manager of the theatre he had the humble inglorious job of resident author—similar, perhaps, to the job of script-writer in a radio or television studio today. He was on tap, so to speak; if a new play was wanted, if a scene had to be rewritten before it was actable, if an epidemic of bad colds made it necessary to scrap one or two small parts and rearrange the script so that two or three actors could "double" (*i.e.*, play two or more parts), if any crisis arose which could be solved by doctoring the script, Will Shakespeare was the man. If he was not on the premises the manager would know where to find him.

We get a better and fuller conception of Shakespeare if we realise that the brilliant creator of Rosalind and of Lear was equally successful in the less impressive activities of a busy scribe behind the scenes. But we must not expect everything he wrote to be a masterpiece.

# VIII. The Text

By the "text" of Shakespeare we usually mean the form in which the printed plays have come down to us. None of the original manuscripts have survived.

There was no system like the "royalty" system of today by which a playwright could make money by the sale of the book of his play, so Shakespeare himself had no financial interest in such publications. Yet if a play was popular enough there would be people anxious to read it. The printers' (or publishers') problem was how to get hold of the script of the plays.

There were two ways. Some system of shorthand had already been invented and "stenographers", as they were even then called, would attend a performance and scribble down as much of the play as they could. Some of the less important actors might be willing to check over their parts afterwards with the stenographer—for a tip, of course—but most of the shorthand version would go to the printer unchecked. The margin of error was very wide, to say the least. The other method was less liable to error, perhaps. By some means or other, the printer would get hold of a "prompt copy"—a copy of the play used by the prompter. This would have all the alterations and modifications in the text which had been introduced during rehearsals; it would be creased, scored over, heavily marked and occasionally almost illegible except to the prompter himself. The present-day process of proof-reading by the author (or by a skilled proof-reader) was not then adopted and it is obvious that the first editions of these plays, whether Shakespeare's or any other dramatist's, were likely to be full of mistakes of all kinds.

## THE QUARTOS

These individual plays, published separately as pamphlets for about sixpence each, were called Quartos. We can judge the popularity of a play in its own time by the number of Quarto editions the publishers found it profitable to issue, although naturally our information is not complete after all these years. *Richard III* and *Henry IV, Part I* went into six editions. *Richard II* and *Romeo and Juliet* into four. For some of the plays no Quarto editions are known and for several others there was only one.

## THE FIRST FOLIO

In 1623, a few months after the death of Shakespeare's widow, a large volume of 908 folio pages was issued by a printer, William Jaggard, in association with others, entitled "Mr William Shakespeare's Comedies, Histories and Tragedies." This was the famous "First Folio." Five or six hundred copies were printed and over 150 are still known to exist. There were thirty-seven plays, some of which had never before been printed. The editors of the collection were John Heminge and Henry Condell, two old friends of Shakespeare's; they had been fellow-actors with him and he had remembered them in his will ("xxvjs. viiid. a peece to buy them ringes.")

*First Quarto, 1597*

**King.** Vilain Ile make thee fafe, (feare
*Aum.* Stay thy reuengefull hand, thou haſt no cauſe to
*York.* Open the dore, fecure foole, hardie King,
Shall I for loue ſpeake treaſon to thy face,
Open the dore, or I will breake it open.
**King** What is the matter vncle, ſpeake, recouer breath,
Tell vs, how neare is daunger,

*First Folio, 1623*

> *Bul.* Villaine, Ile make thee fafe.
> *Aum.* Stay thy reuengefull hand, thou haſt no cauſe
> to feare.
> *Torke.* Open the doore, fecure foole-hardy King :
> Shall I for loue ſpeake treaſon to thy face?
> Open the doore, or I will breake it open.
> *Enter Torke.*
> *Bul.* What is the matter (Vnkle) ſpeak, recouer breath,
> Tell vs how neere is danger,

*An edition of* 1889

*Boling.* Villain, I'll make thee safe. [*Drawing*
*Aum.* Stay thy revengeful hand; thou hast no cause to fear.
*York* [*within*] Open the door, secure, foolhardy king:
    Shall I for love speak treason to thy face?
    Open the door, or I will break it open.
        [*Bolingbroke opens the door, and afterwards re-locks it.*
          *Enter* YORK
*Boling.* What is the matter, uncle? speak;
    Recover breath; tell us how near is danger.

*'Arden' Edition,* 1956

*Bol.* I'll make thee safe.    [*Draws his sword.*]
*Aum.*                Stay thy revengeful hand,
    Thou hast no cause to fear.
*York.*               Open the door,
    Secure, foolhardy king. Shall I, for love,
    Speak treason to thy face? Open the door,
    Or I will break it open.
           *Enter* YORK
*Bol.*                Uncle, speak,
    Recover breath, tell us how near is danger.

*The Text of Shakespeare: Four versions of some lines from King Richard the Second.*
*The Folio differs slightly from the Quarto; the* 1889 *edition invents new stage directions;*
*in the* 1956 *edition the editor, in the light of modern scholarship, reconstructs the passage*
*as Shakespeare probably intended it to be*

There can be little doubt that the volume was intended as a tribute to his memory, since there was not much to be made out of such a publication and the editors had secured verses from Ben Jonson and others in praise of the author and printed them at the beginning of the book. The printing is not particularly good and there are many errors, but at least here were most of Shakespeare's plays in one volume—for the first time.

Several of the plays had never, as far as we know, appeared previously in print, but the editors used a Quarto version of a play when there was one available. It is not surprising that the Folio text is as inaccurate and "corrupt", as the book-men say, as the Quartos.

### SINCE THE FIRST FOLIO

Ever since 1623, or soon after, editors and scholars have been trying to improve on the Quarto and Folio text of Shakespeare's plays. They have compared different texts, where they exist, both with each other and with the text of other works which appeared at about the same date; they have studied the handwriting of the period; and they have applied commonsense and "detection". There have been some remarkable solutions, one of which will illustrate the kind of work which the scholars are always doing.

In *Henry V* the "Hostess" of a tavern is describing the death of Sir John Falstaff. In the Quarto editions her words, at one point, are:

His nose was as sharp as a pen . . .
I knew there was no way but one.

In the Folio, however, her words at this point are:

I knew there was but one way, for
his nose was as sharp as a pen and
a Table of green fields . . .

Obviously that doesn't make sense and for many years the scholars were baffled. Then one of them made a brilliant suggestion. Either the shorthand-writer had mis-heard the actor, or he had "read back" his shorthand incorrectly; what the lady really said was:

. . . his nose was as sharp as a pen
and a' babbled of green fields . . .

(The use of *a'*, for *he*, was common among uneducated people.)

It was only a suggestion, but it was so logical that most editors have adopted it. But there are still many obviously incorrect or highly suspicious words and phrases in Shakespeare which the editors have so far not been able to explain away; the work goes on all the time.

*Shakespeare's signature to his will (Somerset House)*

# IX. "For All Time"

So far we have been considering mainly the facts about Shakespeare, with a little speculation thrown in here and there. But no writer was less understood or enjoyed on a mere study of facts. Shakespeare was a great poet and a great playwright; but he was something more. Even this brief survey of his life and work must have shown that his greatness was not to be measured by the same standards as we apply to other poets and dramatists.

One of the first to recognise his stature was his friend and contemporary, Ben Jonson. He was eight years younger than Shakespeare and much more of a scholar. He might have been expected to envy Shakespeare's success and as a matter of fact there are evidences of rivalry between these two dramatists. But when Shakespeare's First Folio was published Ben Jonson was among those who contributed tributes to the author. In the course of a poem of about 80 lines, in which he addresses Shakespeare as

> The applause! delight! the wonder of our Stage!

he says also

> He was not of an age, but for all time!

Now, making allowances for the language of flattery which is proper to a tribute of this kind, this was certainly a bold pronouncement. Jonson meant, more or less, that Shakespeare was not one of those who are honoured only in his day but that his fame would last *for all time*. As it happened, Jonson was a true prophet.

SHAKESPEARE'S KNOWLEDGE OF HUMAN NATURE

We have seen that in his knowledge of the human heart he was greater than his own generation. His audiences would have preferred a Shylock whom they could have wholeheartedly despised, a Richard III whom they could hate or a King John whom they could admire without reserve; but he knew that people are not made that way, that even the worst villains have some spark of good in them and that no man or woman is without fault. That is only one aspect of his wisdom, however. He seemed to know instinctively how people would react to any set circumstances, what they would say and how they would feel. This was as true of Beatrice or Imogen or Cleopatra as it was of his male characters— and that is part of the miracle.

Shakespeare's women are all amazingly true to life. You have only to compare them with the women characters of almost any other novelist or dramatist to realise how they stand out as living, *real* personalities, not cardboard figures invented by the author, given a name and then set down among the other characters to say their lines.

The result is that we have a sort of Portrait Gallery of Shakespearean characters—Falstaff, Portia, Henry V, Hamlet, Rosalind, Malvolio, Othello, and so on. Besides these heroes and heroines there are the hundreds of minor characters— Pistol, Osric, Kent, Enobarbus, Casca, Celia, Sir Andrew Aguecheek, Titania and the rest, all of whom we seem to know personally as soon as we meet them. Only Dickens has provided us with so many imaginary creations who have become household words.

It is not possible to separate what a poet says from the way he says it; that must never be forgotten. We know and love these inventions of Shakespeare's because of the words in which they are presented to us or in which they present themselves; we feel as Shakespeare felt, we rejoice or mourn or suffer or love in sympathy with his characters because of the language Shakespeare used and the way in which he used it. It is often poetic; it is often dramatic; but the poetry and the drama are all part of the whole thing. You cannot (except in the songs) pick out a line of poetry or a dramatic phrase and say it is a typical piece of Shakespearean poetry or dramatic force; the poetry or the dramatic force are part and parcel of the play, they cannot be separated.

There are plenty of examples to choose from. One that springs to the mind is not in verse at all; it is Henry V's talk to his soldiers in Act IV, Scene i. Look it up now and read it—and imagine while you are reading it that you can hear it being spoken on the stage. Even if you have no ear for the beauty of good prose (and there is nothing to be ashamed of if you haven't and nothing to be proud of if you have: these are "God's gifts," as Dogberry says in *Much Ado*)—even if you cannot recognise the sweetly balanced rhythm of the prose you must *feel* that this is good strong English, the sort of English that Henry, being the man he is,

would speak. Shakespeare did not write the speech and fit it into the play; he put himself as nearly as he could in Henry's place and wrote what he thought in those circumstances Henry would say.

Or take a few verse quotations. In *King John* (Act IV, Scene iii) the body of the boy Arthur has been found dead by the castle walls. Faulconbridge suspects that Hubert has killed him but Hubert indignantly declares his innocence, whereupon Faulconbridge says "Go, bear him in thine arms." There are no stage directions here in most editions but we can see what happens. Faulconbridge knows Hubert, and he knows that if he did kill Arthur he would be unable to lift the child's dead body—his conscience would not allow him to. But Hubert steps forward and picks up the boy in his arms; whereupon Faulconbridge says

> How easy dost thou take all England up!

It is a beautiful line—simple enough, as beauty usually is, but full of tenderness and meaning. It tells us all we want to know about both the men, and it is at the same time pure dramatic poetry.

In *The Winter's Tale*, King Leontes, who thinks his wife is dead, is remembering her eyes. He says

> Stars, stars,
> And all eyes else dead coals!

In *Twelfth Night* Viola, pretending to be a man, is asked by Olivia—with whom she is in love—what she would do if the one she loved refused to see her; and Viola replies

> Make me a willow cabin at your gate
> And call upon my soul within the house. . . .

So we might go on quoting examples, and each one would tell the same story—that the poetry in Shakespeare is not something *applied*, like a sparkling necklace or a coat of paint, but rises naturally and spontaneously as part of the character and the drama.

### HOUSEHOLD WORDS

Somebody is supposed to have said of *Hamlet* that it is "full of quotations"—which is one way of saying that many of Shakespeare's phrases and expressions have become familiar sayings. "Every inch a king," "Alone I did it," "Once more unto the breach," "What's in a name?" "Brave new world," "A Daniel come to judgement," "Lay on, Macduff," —there must be literally hundreds of these phrases which we use or hear every day of our lives without knowing, even, that they were first written by William Shakespeare over three hundred years ago. No other proof is required, surely, that he has become part of our inheritance.

### SHAKESPEARE'S SONGS

If he had left us only his lyrics we should still have to acknowledge Shakespeare as a great poet. They are scattered all through the plays and at least a score of them are as well known and loved today as they were when they were written. Many people believe "Fear no more the heat o' the sun," in *Cymbeline*, to be the loveliest of them all; better known are "O mistress mine," (*Twelfth Night*), "Where the bee sucks," (*The Tempest*), and "Who is Sylvia?" (*Two Gentlemen of Verona*). But everybody has his or her own favourite. Many of them, of course, owe their lasting popularity partly to their musical setting, but Shakespeare has always attracted the great composers. Mendelssohn's Overture and Incidental Music to *The Midsummer Night's Dream*, Nicolai's "Merry Wives of Windsor" Overture, Elgar's portrait in music of Falstaff, Tchaikovsky's *Romeo and Juliet* are but a few of the best-known examples. It is also worth noting here that the Italian composer, Verdi, at the height of his greatness, turned to the plays of Shakespeare for some of his most magnificent operas—*Othello, Macbeth, Falstaff*.

### "FOR ALL TIME"

It is because of this unequalled combination of rare gifts—his sympathy, his knowledge of the human heart, his command of poetic and dramatic English, his ability to create characters, his humour, his musical songs—that Shakespeare has kept his hold on people's affections. In the late seventeenth century, it is true, he was not fully understood and his plays were sadly altered and "revised". But at all other times his plays have been popular. There is an entirely false idea that they are "highbrow" and that it is not possible to enjoy them on the stage unless one is a scholar or has at least studied them at school. The facts disprove this. In the seventeenth century a ship's captain produced two plays, one of which was *Hamlet,* for his own and two other crews, to entertain them when they were idle. In both of the great wars of the twentieth century, performances of Shakespeare's plays have been received with delight by ordinary men and women in the Services stationed far away from cinemas and dance-halls. All over the

English-speaking world schools have been presenting Shakespeare's plays on festive occasions, and although both children and parents have been apprehensive at first they have always been spell-bound in the end, often to their own amazement!

Let us be honest. There *are* difficulties. One of them is the language, which abounds in obsolete words, abbreviations like "to 't" for "to it," "in 't" for "in it," and worse, and strange constructions like "whereof the ewe not bites." Another is that Shakespeare, writing for a contemporary audience, did just what playwrights do today; he introduced contemporary references, many of which are meaningless to modern audiences. A third is that, in the Histories especially, there are often a number of characters who have similar names or titles (and sometimes even change them in the course of the play) and who tend to land us in desperate confusion. The amazing thing is that after a little while one no longer notices these things. The language difficulty remains, but who can swear that he hears and understands every word, first time, in even a modern play? The contemporary references pass over our heads or, more often, are wisely "cut" by the producer. And the confused characters steadily sort themselves out.

It is in times of stress and anxiety that people most appreciate Shakespeare; he has the answer to many problems and even if he had not he would still provide solace and distraction. What is true of individuals is true also of nations and it is no coincidence that Shakespeare's plays have enjoyed a great wave of popularity during the last twenty years.

## SHAKESPEARE FILMED

Whether the wave of popularity has encouraged the filming of Shakespeare's plays or *vice versa* is not certain; experiments in the 'twenties and 'thirties were not particularly successful and it looks as if the more recent films have been made to meet the new demand. Opinions on these films are naturally divided. There will always be some people who insist on the necessity for presenting Shakespeare as it was written, and since it was not written for the films these people are offended, and even shocked. On the other side are those who feel that the cinema attracts millions compared with the theatre's thousands and this introduction of so vast an audience to Shakespeare cannot do harm to the poet and should be good for the millions. Perhaps the greatest danger is that producers and directors may feel it necessary to simplify or dilute Shakespeare drastically in order to meet the modern cinema patrons halfway. There is a story of a girl who was overheard telling her friend that she would have enjoyed the film of *Julius Caesar* more if it had been in English instead of Shakespearean—which sums up the difficulty very neatly. But the girl was wrong, of course; had she known it, she would have enjoyed the film a great deal less if it had not adhered to the language of Shakespeare.

## RADIO AND TELEVISION

Although Shakespeare did not write for the films he might easily have been writing for sound radio! Only when we are unable to see the actors, only when we are free (with the minimum assistance from a narrator) to make our own picture in our minds of what is going on, can we approach the perfect twentieth-century appreciation of Shakespeare. With nothing to come between us and the poet's mind but the sounds coming from the radio set we are free to let those sounds do their work unaided; if the music and other effects are not too insistent and if the radio actors are sincere and competent we have the best chance, since Shakespeare's own audiences, of getting the best out of his plays.

Television is another matter. It offers none of the detachment of the silent radio and only a partial imitation of the spectacle which is possible on stage or film. None the less, "T.V. Shakespeare" is to be welcomed; like the film, it can do little harm to Shakespeare and may do much good to the viewers.

### SHAKESPEARE IN SCHOOL

Until quite recently Shakespeare was not often read in schools. A few plays were studied—mainly because they were set in examinations—but the process was sadly different from reading and if any enjoyment resulted from the study it was almost accidental. Outside the few "safe" plays the main body of his work was a sealed book. The "safe" plays were *As You Like It*, the *Merchant*, *Twelfth Night* and the *Dream* among the comedies, *Henry V* and *Richard II* among the histories, and *Macbeth*. For older boys and girls there was *Hamlet*, *Julius Caesar* and possibly *Coriolanus*. In the course of their schooling few students read more

than two or three of these ten. They were forced to learn about the contemporary references and the meaning of obscure phrases or obsolete words; they memorised brief character-sketches of the main characters and lists of anachronisms; and they got by heart the "best" long speeches.

Conditions are changing. Examiners tend to ask fewer and fewer questions based on the kind of textual commentary which filled most of the school editions of the plays; teachers are therefore more free to arouse their pupils' enthusiasm for the dramatic and poetic excellencies; and the boys and girls themselves are showing that they are both able and eager to tackle Shakespeare "neat"— even those passages and those plays which used to be considered too difficult or too outspoken. Genius speaks to all people, at all levels.

Best of all is that few schools now close their eyes to the essential fact that Shakespeare was written to be acted. Instead of the select few who are to take part in the annual play, whole classes now *act* the play they are studying—a scene here, a whole act there, a page or two now and then—and they are discovering in this way that the so-called difficulties disappear like magic when the words on the page are translated into action.

The theatre, the film, radio, television, the class-room, the library—never was Shakespeare so popular; never was Ben Jonson so amply justified. "He was not of an age, but for all time."

# A SELECT BOOK LIST

By ELIZABETH N. BEWICK, A.L.A.

BOAS, GUY. *Shakespeare and the young actor: a guide to production*. Rockliff, 1955. Illus. Personal reminiscences of productions at Sloane School, with practical advice to other would-be producers.

BROWN, IVOR. *Shakespeare*. Collins, 1949. An attempt to assess Shakespeare the man, as revealed in his writings.

CHUTE, MARCHETTE. *Shakespeare and his stage*. U.L.P., repr., 1954. Illus. A brief study of Shakespeare and the Tudor theatre: how his plays were devised, dressed, rehearsed and received in his own day.

*Shakespeare of London*. Secker & Warburg, 1951. Book list. A biographical study and an attempt at a reconstruction of the London of Shakespeare's day.

ELLIS, RUTH. *The Shakespeare memorial theatre*. Winchester Pubs., 1948. Illus. A history of the Stratford-on-Avon Memorial Theatre from its inception to 1948.

HALLIDAY, F. E. *The enjoyment of Shakespeare*. Duckworth, 1952. Illus. An introduction to the reading of Shakespeare's plays for pleasure.

*A Shakespeare companion*. Duckworth, 1952. Illus. Book list. An alphabetical reference book and encyclopaedia, covering Shakespeare's life and works, the theatre of his day and the production of his plays from Elizabethan times to the present day.

*Shakespeare: a pictorial biography*. Thames & Hudson, 1953. Illus. A beautifully-produced book with illustrations ranging from photographs of Stratford to facsimile reproductions of Elizabethan records. Useful for reference as well as general reading.

HARRISON, G. B. *Introducing Shakespeare*. Penguin Books, repr. 1957. Illus. Book list. A background book to the Penguin Shakespeare and an introduction to the biographical and critical study of the man and his plays.

HODGES, C. WALTER. *Shakespeare and the players*. Benn, 1948. Illus. An introduction to the study of Shakespeare's plays as they were acted in his day, with a reconstruction of the structure of the Globe theatre.

RALEIGH, SIR WALTER, and others, *eds. Shakespeare's England: an account of the life and manners of his age*. 2 vols. Oxford, Clarendon Press, repr. 1932. Illus. A collection of essays by authoritative writers on all aspects of life in Shakespeare's day. Advanced.

WILSON, JOHN DOVER, *eds. Life in Shakespeare's England: a book of Elizabethan prose*. C.U.P., repr. 1920, also Penguin Books, repr. 1954. An anthology for the student and the general reader, in an attempt to portray the social life of Shakespeare's time and the background against which his plays were produced.

TEXTS. There are many collected editions of the plays, from the beautifully produced *New Nonesuch Shakespeare* in 4 volumes to the single-volume *Oxford Shakespeare*, but collected editions tend either towards bulk or smallness of print. The individual plays are available in such pocket editions as the *Penguin Shakespeare* and the *New Temple Shakespeare* (Dent), and these can be collected as one needs them.

| | | | |
|---|---|---|---|
| 1560–70 | '64 Shakespeare born | '64 Marlowe born | |
| 1570–80 | '72 } Spent a few years at Stratford-on-Avon<br>'77 } Grammar School (?) | '72 Massacre of St Bartholomew<br>'77 } Drake's voyage round<br>'80 } the world | Elizabeth I: 1558–1603 |
| 1580–90 | '82 } Shakespeare married<br><br>} The "Lost Years" | '87 { Drake singes the King of Spain's beard<br>Mary Q. of Scots beheaded<br>'88 Defeat of Armada<br>'90 Loss of "The Revenge" | |
| 1590–1600 | '91 } First Plays<br>'94 } Poems<br>'95 } Second Period (M.N.D., M. of V., R. II, Hy. IV, Hy. V)<br>'98 }<br>'99 } The Great Comedies<br>'01 }<br>'02 } | '93 { Death of Marlowe<br>Plague in London<br><br>'97 } Globe Theatre built<br>'98 } | |
| 1600–10 | } The Great Tragedies<br><br>'09 } | '01 Essex's rebellion<br>'03 Death of Elizabeth I<br>'05 Gunpowder Plot<br>'08 { Blackfriars Theatre opened | James I: 1603–25 |
| 1610–20 | '10 } Last Plays<br>'11 } Shakespeare retired to Stratford-on-Avon<br><br>'16 Shakespeare died<br><br>'23 First Folio | '11 Authorized Version of English Bible<br>'12 Globe Theatre burnt down<br>'18 Raleigh executed<br>'19 30 Years' War begins | |

*Time Chart*

# INDEX

*All for Love* (Dryden), 47
*All's Well that End's Well*, 29, 53
*Antony and Cleopatra*, 18, 20, 47–8
Arden, Forest of, 19
Arden, Mary, 10, 20
*As You Like It*, 20, 26, 27–8, 36, 49, 61

Bacon, Sir Francis, 3, 18
bear-baiting, 4
Blackfriars Theatre, 19, 8 (footnote)
Brown, Mr Ivor, 18, 47
Burbage, 15

Cecil, Lord, 3
Chamberlain, the Lord, 6, 15, 17, 32, 33
Charlecote, 13
*Comedy of Errors, The*, 17, 22
Condell, Henry, 54
*Coriolanus*, 20, 26, 48–9, 61
*Cymbeline*, 50, 59

Derby, Earl of, 18
Drake, Sir Francis, 3, 30
drama before Shakespeare, 5
Dryden, 47
Dyer, Sir Edward, 18

Elizabeth I, 2, 3, 30, 32
Essex, Earl of, 32

Falstaff, 25, 33–4, 57, 59
Field, Richard, 14
films, Shakespeare in, 60
Fletcher, John, 52
Folio, First, 54, 56, 57

Globe Theatre, 19, 52
Greene, Robert, 13, 17

Hall, Dr, 12

*Hamlet*, 17, 20, 29, 40–2, 53, 59
Hathaway, Anne, 12
Hawkins, 3
Hemminge, John, 54
Henry VIII, 31
Holinshed, 16, 43, 45
Hooker, 3

Inns of Court, 5, 6

Jaggard, 54
James I, 2, 3, 17, 45
Jonson, Ben, 15, 57
*Julius Caesar*, 38–40, 47, 49, 61

Kempe, 15
*King Henry IV, Part I*, 33, 54
    *Part II*, 34–5
*King Henry V*, 35–6, 56, 58, 61
*King Henry VI*, 17, 53
*King Henry VIII*, 52
*King John*, 31, 57, 58
*King Lear*, 5, 20, 43–5
King's Men, The, 6, 17

Leicester, Earl of, 12
London, 2, 3, 4, 5, 6, 13, 14, 20
Lopez, Dr, 25
*Love's Labour's Lost*, 17, 22
*Lucrece*, 14, 17, 19
Lucy, Sir Thomas, 13

*Macbeth*, 4, 8, 16, 20, 45–7, 59, 61
Maddermarket Theatre, 53
Magna Carta, 32
Marlowe, Christopher, 18, 31
Mary Tudor, Queen, 2, 31
masques, 5, 52 (footnote)
*Measure for Measure*, 29, 53
*Merchant of Venice, The*, 24–5, 61